Flirting 101

—

Flirting 101

How to Charm Your Way to Love, Friendship, and Success

Michelle Lia Lewis and Andrew Bryant

Thomas Dunne Books
St. Martin's Griffin
New York

THOMAS DUNNE BOOKS.
An imprint of St. Martin's Press.

www.stmartins.com

Illustrations by Jane Cameron, Fisheye Design, reprinted with permission.

Photo of Michelle Lia Lewis by Graeme Gillies.

Photo of Andrew Bryant courtesy of author's private collection.

ISBN 0-312-33412-5
EAN 978-0312-33412-3

First published in Australia by Allen & Unwin in 2003

10 9 8 7 6 5 4

Contents

Preface

Our first challenge in writing this book was to sift
through what seemed like ad hoc techniques and
urban myths to devise a flirting method that could be
easily communicated and applied. Many of the people we
observed and interviewed had no conscious understanding
about how they flirted, they just did their best.

We found that although flirting is a much broader
pursuit than dating, and has more variety in its purposes
and outcomes, great flirts always have a positive attitude
and put the other person first. Now that might sound easy
to do, and it is, so long as you know how. Our experience
had certainly shown us, through thousands of case studies,
what was happening when people flirted, but now we had
to work out the "why" and the "how" of the task. By the
time we finished the research and writing we saw flirting
in quite a different light.

Right now you may be thinking that flirting is friv-
olous, without much use past attracting somebody's
attention. But you'll discover in this book that flirting has
many far-reaching uses that go beyond getting a date or

even being romantic. At its simplest, flirting is fun and entertaining. It's a feel-good activity. However, it also has the potential to be complex and political.

Although we had never collaborated before, we decided to combine our experience to write this book. We each brought what we thought was complementary knowledge to the project but, initially at least, all we had was an idea. Had my husband, Fraser, not pitched the idea and got a warm and enthusiastic response from Jo Paul, our publisher at Allen & Unwin, we might never have continued to explore and research the nature of flirting. And we would not have succeeded in finishing the book if it had not been for Jo Paul's understanding, encouragement, savvy, and wit. Then it was the turn of our very talented U.S. editor, Carolyn Chu at St. Martin's Press, who saw potential, translated our Aussie slang, and kept the spirit alive.

With this book our goal has been to take you to the point where you feel confident you can be a great flirt and where you can use your flirting skills in many varied situations. The real joy for us is in teaching you how to get the flirting attitude so you can feel confident to get out there and practice. When you are out there please remember our golden rule: If it isn't fun, it isn't flirting.

ONE

What Is Flirting?

The meeting of two personalities is like the contact of two chemical substances; if there's any reaction, both are transformed.

C. G. Jung

The History of Flirting

In the Victorian era flirting was considered an art form. It was such a large part of socializing that young women, being groomed for marriage, were taught how to flirt using fashion accessories as props, and men were schooled in recognizing these flirtatious signals. The established signals and patterns of flirting leaned heavily on the use of personal items—fans, gloves, handkerchiefs, parasols—to convey interest or disinterest. For example, when a woman fanned herself slowly it indicated she was either married or engaged; to fan quickly showed independence. To say yes, the woman rested the fan on her right cheek; on her left cheek for no. Fanning with the right hand in front of the face was a message to the man, "Come on, follow me," and the rapid opening and closing of the fan was a signal that she wanted to be kissed.

The use of the fan, gloves or parasol was a way of sending messages that were always well understood because everyone knew the language of flirting. Our modern day flirting signals, such as winking, playing with your hair, looking steadily at someone, crossing your legs or touching the person you are talking to, were once all considered the height of rudeness. The rules governing social etiquette in the nineteenth century were very strict and rigid. A man could not speak to a woman unless he had been formally introduced, even if they were at the same social event; however flirting of the accepted kind at social events was not only permitted, it was encouraged.

Flirting throughout the nineteenth and early twentieth centuries was a social art as well as an art for doing business. While the use of the term "schmoozing" might be considered modern, the idea certainly isn't. Business dealings, such as negotiating a loan, a sale or a contract, were traditionally conducted by a series of social events where much time was spent talking and getting to know each other and the respective families before deciding to do business.

By the 1960s, the art of flirting was replaced by free love and people found new ways to "connect" with each other. The dynamics between men and women changed and with these changes flirting and courtship were re-defined. While the lines remained blurred for the next 40 years, flirting never died out, although it did get forgotten and somewhat overwhelmed by sexual impatience and the modern definition of courtship. The faster paced our lives became, the more we looked for deep and meaningful connections with others, and the harder we worked in our jobs, the more we craved fun in our social lives.

Flirting has always been a fun way to connect with others so it's no wonder that in the twenty-first century flirting is making a triumphant return. Every day you meet people, some you know, some you don't, some you'll want to know and some you won't. The quality of your life is often determined by the quality of these interactions. This book is about flirting, about the attitude and skills needed to successfully flirt. Flirting is a wonderful thing, bringing energy to your daily interactions and improving your life; whether by getting you a better table at a restaurant, a smile from a stranger or meeting your soul mate.

When you flirt with someone you are actually paying them a compliment. It shows them that you have noticed them. You probably already have your own opinions about what flirting means to you, but in this book we are going to share with you our research and what we think flirting is.

Flirting is like dancing. One person leads while the other has the choice to follow or not. If they choose to follow, there is a rhythmic flow of energy where both people benefit.

Flirting is fun, playful and energetic. Everyone involved gets to feel good about themselves. It can be a useful way of getting what you want in a way that makes people happy to give it to you.

Because true flirting is ambiguous, you can always get away with it anywhere. When you say something flirtatiously it is fun, but the same line delivered with a sexual motive can sound sleazy and puts people off. The moment flirting moves from ambiguity to the obvious it crosses the line from flirtation to seduction.

Seduction is about power or sex or both. Flirting, a playful energy, is about making the other person feel good. Flirting can, of course, be a prelude to seduction and from time to time you may want to cross the line. After reading this book you will be able to do just that with knowledge and style.

Knowing where the line is will protect you from ending up in bed with someone you really only wanted to talk to, or from making a terrible mistake in work situations. Untrained flirts often fall into these traps because they don't recognize the difference between chatting to and chatting up. You will.

Flirting is like public speaking; some people seem to be born with the skill, others have to learn it. The end result, though, is the same—an ability to attract and hold other people's interest.

Anybody can learn to be a good flirt, it takes just three things: the right attitude, knowing the techniques of the art and applying those techniques. You've watched other people flirt with style and admired them for it. Now it's your turn to find out how and be able to do it yourself. Welcome to the world of flirting.

In this book you'll find the five attitudes and seven skills you'll need to become a great flirt. And take note, with flirting it's all in the delivery.

Drew walks into his regular coffee shop. It's quiet, and there's a very attractive woman picking up some takeout.

"Hi, Drew," calls out Sam, the coffee maker. "How are you today?"

"Sensational," says Drew with grin.

"How come you get to be sensational?" asks the girl at the counter.

"Well I could tell you but . . . " He pauses.

"But you'd have to kill me?" she replies.

"But it would be more fun for you to find out," says Drew.

"You still haven't answered my question," says the girl, maintaining her composure and pretending to ignore the flirt.

"Let me ask you a question," says Drew. "How's your day?"

"All right."

"So what would it take to move it from all right to great?" asks Drew, gesturing an improvement with his hands.

"Well, it depends on what happens."

"Really," replies Drew with a tinge of sarcasm. "I thought it's not what happens to you but how you handle it."

"Maybe you're right." She ponders.

"My name's Drew. What's yours?"

"Kristen."

"Listen, Kristen, if you would like to talk more about this, here's my card."

Kristen takes Drew's card.

"Do you have a card?"

"Sure," she says and she gives it to him.

"If I haven't heard from you in a couple of days can I give you a call?"

"Yes, okay," says Kristen and leaves.

"Wow," says Sam, who has been watching and listening to the whole exchange. "That was smooth. That's the fastest I have ever seen anybody get a number, and you knew just what to say."

The Flirting Attitude

Zig Ziglar, the motivational speaker, is fond of saying: "It's not your aptitude but your attitude that determines your altitude."

Drew got to flirt with Kristen because he had a great attitude toward life and having a good attitude is attractive. Being good looking or clever with words is worthless if your attitude sucks.

Your attitude depends on your state of mind and through our research and experience we have identified five states of mind that make up a great flirting attitude. Adopting a good flirtatious attitude and applying it to the skills you will learn will ensure you become a truly great flirt.

The five states of mind or attitudes are:

- playfulness
- fun
- taking notice

- loving people
- go for it.

In turn each of these attitudes contain certain ingredients:

- playfulness—light-hearted, high-spirited, mischievous, frisky, teasing
- fun—witty, entertaining, lively, willing to play the game
- taking notice—observing, aware of the other person, showing an interest
- loving people—appreciation, acceptance, curiosity, gregarious, social
- go for it—taking risks, liberated, optimistic, opportunistic.

Being playful and light-hearted makes the flirting safe but allows for a little naughtiness. Using fun attracts people, they are drawn to the energy. Taking notice allows the flirt to learn about the other person and show an interest, making them feel special and appreciated.

Our research has shown that great flirts have a lot of friends of the opposite sex. Great flirts love people—male flirts love and have an affinity for women; female flirts love and have an understanding of men. Flirts also know how to go for it. They are not afraid to take risks because they have let go of past hurts and are optimistic about themselves and other people.

Go back to the story of Drew and Kristen and spot how Drew's states of mind gave him the right attitude for flirting.

There was a study done with kids learning to play basketball. The researchers divided the kids up into two groups. One group got to go straight on the court and start shooting hoops. The other group had to sit out on the sideline but were instructed to visualize the ball going in the hoop—how they would need to stand and how they would need to feel to get the ball in the hoop. They were also told to believe they could get that ball in the hoop. Both groups were then asked to take a series of shots at the hoop. The group that had been practicing did pretty well but the group that had been sitting on the sideline getting their attitude right, well, they blitzed it.

You can change your attitude by changing what you think and how you feel. To be playful you just have to think playful and feel playful. If you don't particularly feel playful right now, think back to a time when you did. Notice what you were thinking and feeling then. Become aware of how just thinking of a time when you were acting playful causes you to feel playful now.

Another way of getting the right attitude is to imagine what it would be like to already be there. If you were going to be playful, how would you stand, how would you breathe, what would you be thinking?

When you are feeling playful you are light-hearted, high-spirited, mischievous, frisky and teasing. How would you be if you were feeling like this?

The same process works for the other four attitudes. Fun is similar to playfulness. Taking notice is when you turn up your senses so that you can tune in to people. To love people, think of those people you already accept and really appreciate—how do you feel when you are around them? Now imagine looking at everybody you meet in the same way.

Have you ever been in a situation where you just went for it? You had nothing to lose and everything to gain, your heart and mind both agreed that this was the right thing to do and you were the right person to do it. This is the "go for it" state of mind and it is the way great flirts live.

In the next chapter there are some great exercises for getting the right attitude and being in the mood to flirt.

Seven Skills of a Great Flirt

Once you have the right attitude you can learn and develop the skills. We'll expand on the skills in the coming chapters and have included plenty of exercises for you to become a master flirt, but for now here is a list and a short explanation:

- market yourself
- choosing when
- get in step
- insight
- word power
- out of sight
- make 'em feel good.

Great flirts know how to market themselves: they just know how to present themselves to be attractive and appealing. Flirts also have a good sense of time and place and so they can choose when to flirt. To flirt successfully you have to make contact and create rapport, which is the skill we call get in step. Insight is the ability to read and understand non-verbal flirting signals. Word power is about knowing what to say to create the right impact. Flirts don't need to be face to face; by using technology they can be out of sight to make the first move or to stay in touch, keeping the energy flowing. Flirts have the ability to make people feel good and link that feeling back to themselves.

Great Flirting Personalities

There are many famous people who have flirtatious personalities. Some of them have been on the top-ten lists of sexiest men and women of their time and all of them have one thing in common; they have captured our attention through the flirtatious signals they give off to a crowd at large. It doesn't matter that we have never been within a bull's roar of them, we somehow feel their energy is directed at us and for us.

Bill Clinton, with his soft southern accent and the way a smile always plays around his mouth, is one of the famous flirting personalities. Nicole Kidman is a wonderful example of the playful flirt. Her voice has an innocent girlish quality, her eye contact is candid one minute and fluttering the next. She comes across as clever—with a wink. George Clooney consistently flirts his way through the media circus that follows him. His laid-back attitude is punctuated with the most dazzling smile that lights up his entire face, and the smile seems to be meant just for you.

Sean Connery is a great flirt and is still considered one of the sexiest men alive. He is a master at making the sort of eye contact that appears to exclude everybody else. He engages with his eyes and holds you captive. As a contrast, the other actors selected to play James Bond have been chosen because they are stylish, sophisticated and seductive. Sean Connery is this . . . and more. Also note, the Bond character often crosses the line and uses seduction rather than flirting to get what he wants.

So How Do You Feel About Flirting?

If you have read this far then it's fair to assume you are either interested in learning how to flirt or in improving your existing talent. This being so, the first step is to take a look at your existing beliefs about flirting. Flirting is one of those words that can create heated discussions between people. How you behave is dependent on what you believe so take the following quiz and flush out what it is you believe about flirting.

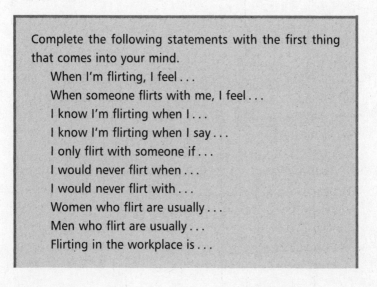

Complete the following statements with the first thing that comes into your mind.

When I'm flirting, I feel . . .

When someone flirts with me, I feel . . .

I know I'm flirting when I . . .

I know I'm flirting when I say . . .

I only flirt with someone if . . .

I would never flirt when . . .

I would never flirt with . . .

Women who flirt are usually . . .

Men who flirt are usually . . .

Flirting in the workplace is . . .

Now answer the following questions.
    When you think of flirting, what do you think of?
    Would you call yourself a flirt?
    What area of your flirting would you like to improve?

Have you answered all the questions? It's important
you answer the questions before you read on because when
you understand your attitudes and beliefs you will be a
better flirt.

We'd like to share with you the various responses we
have had from our research into people's beliefs about
flirting:

When I flirt I feel . . . excited, alive, free, mischievous,
cheeky, playful, adventurous, sexy, and sometimes even
a little naughty.

When someone is flirting with me, I feel . . . happy,
energized, pumped, attractive, flattered, exhilarated,
aroused, happy, good about myself, admired, liked and
appreciated.

I know I am flirting when I . . . try to get someone's
attention, become animated, get aroused, spend a lot
of time talking to someone, notice little things about
someone, get shy, am flippant, try hard.

I only flirt with someone if I . . . feel the other person
is receptive, find them attractive, feel some chemistry

or rapport, feel they are open to it, want them to like me, want them to feel good about themselves, trust them, like them, feel comfortable with them, want to be with them, want them to notice me.

I would never flirt with . . . someone who was married or has a partner, a friend's partner, an ex-partner, a work colleague, someone I don't like, someone I didn't know, a friend of my partner.

Women who usually flirt are . . . confident, shallow, enticing, self-assured, fun to be around, outgoing, usually testing the waters, aware of their sexuality and know how to use it, usually wanting something from the man.

Men who flirt are . . . fun, wanting to know if the woman is receptive, looking to hook up, gregarious, trying very hard, not fun for other men to be around, confident, sleazy, entertaining.

As you can see, people have conflicting views about flirting. Take the woman who feels cheeky when she flirts—she also feels admired and liked when someone flirts with her but thinks women who flirt are usually shallow and men who flirt are often sleazy. Did you have any conflicting or out-of-date beliefs? Do you have any rules, such as it's okay to flirt at a party but not at work?

Conflicting beliefs about flirting are not unusual but like other attitudes that hold you back they'll prevent you from becoming a master flirt. As you read this book and do the exercises we hope you will find flirting to be a fun, energizing and natural way to live.

Flirting Is a Game

"No mind games." You have undoubtedly heard this comment before. Most people are afraid of, or say they don't like playing, "mind games." It seems we are looking for openness and honesty in communication, for the agendas to be clear and uncomplicated. The problem is, we are constantly playing games in our own mind: "Will I or won't I?" "Should I or shouldn't I?" and so on, and strictly speaking every encounter with another person is a game.

John Nash, the brilliant mathematician who lacked any social skills, was portrayed in the movie *A Beautiful Mind*, which provided a wonderful example of what not to do. In the movie he approached a woman in a bar and said, "I don't know exactly what I'm required to say in order for you to have intercourse with me, but can we assume I have said all that, and essentially we're talking about fluid exchange, so can we go straight to the sex?" Her reply, not surprisingly, was to slap him.

A flirt would never do this because they enjoy the "game" of flirting. If you are interested in somebody, flirting with them lets you gauge their response and their level of interest in you. Flirting can be like putting your toe in the water to check the temperature instead of diving straight in and getting a surprise.

Your beliefs and attitude about flirting set the rules and boundaries about where it's safe or not safe to go, basically where the line is. In fact your beliefs and attitudes create the rules of all the games you play in life.

Would you like to learn how to set the stage for flirting with someone and how to play the flirting game? Then read on. Learn the rules, practice some drills and develop winning strategies. The right flirting attitude makes this game fun and safe, because the flirt notices others and genuinely cares for people.

Are You a Flirt?

Do you find it easy to talk to people you don't know?
Do you enjoy watching people?
Do you naturally give compliments?
Do you always try to make eye contact with others?
Are you tactile?
Do you pick up vibes from others?
Can you tell when someone is interested in you?
Can you put a smile on someone's face?

Key Points

- Flirting is playful energy.
- Flirting is a compliment.
- Flirting is fun.
- Flirting is communicating.
- Flirting is ambiguous, not obvious.
- To flirt well you need to have the right attitude.
- Flirting is a game.

TWO

In the Mood

Men are not influenced by things but by their thoughts about things.

Epictetus

D o you have to be in the mood to flirt?" asked one of our seminar participants. "Of course," we replied. "But realize you can choose what mood to be in at any time."

Flirting makes you feel good but you have to feel good to flirt. Does that sound circular? It is.

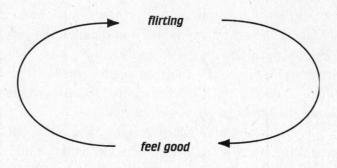

You Choose Your Mood

"Damn rain," Kelly muttered as she stared out of her bedroom window. Her hangover seemed to match the day. Coffee will make me feel better, she thought. She heaved herself out of bed, put on her sloppy sweatshirt and went to the refrigerator.

"Damn," she said when she saw she was out of coffee. "Why does this have to happen to me? The last thing I feel like doing is going out." But then, as she looked through the kitchen window, she said to herself, "It's only rain after all, and I sure need a coffee." She knew she could either sulk around at home all day or just accept the rain and walk to the coffee shop. She made a quick decision. She pulled on her jeans and sneakers and got her coat and umbrella from the closet.

It was better outside than she had imagined. The air was fresh with the scent of wet gardens and the rain made music on the leaves. The cafe was busy when she arrived but there was a table by the door. She claimed it with her coat and umbrella and went to the counter.

"A skinny latte please," she said to the good-looking guy taking the orders. He smiled and repeated the order to the girl operating the coffee machine. He said to Kelly, "Isn't this is a perfect day to sit reading the papers, sipping coffee?" "Yes, I guess it is," she replied, "once you accept the weather and just get out of the house."

Kelly took her latte back to the table. The coffee smelt great, and tasted even better. The cheerful sound of chatting filled the cafe. When she thought about what the guy at the counter had said, her mood shifted. She realized that she appreciated days like this. She had time to herself and the weather couldn't dampen her mood, unless she let it. She was doing what she enjoyed.

Kelly's story illustrates how we can change our mood, attitude or state of mind. How we think and feel depends upon what we focus on. Do you have your mood or does your mood have you?

You always have a state of mind or attitude—the question is, is your attitude attractive or is it more likely to be a turn-off for anybody you come into contact with? You can choose your attitude because you can choose your thoughts, and you might as well choose a good attitude because it will affect the quality of your day, life and relationships.

Taking Control

During any particular day you'll have numerous moods or states of mind; some positive, some intense and some downright ugly. The first step in feeling good and becoming flirtatious is to name your states of mind and to track them. This will give you a clue as to what triggers you positively or negatively.

It doesn't matter what you name your moods as long as you know how they feel. For example, you might wake up in a "groggy state"; realize you are running late and then get into a "frantic state." You get a take-out coffee on the way to the station, smell the aroma and go into a "bliss mood." You get on the train or the bus and "zone out," or you might have a "taking notice attitude" as you people-watch. Get the idea?

The way to track your moods is with a journal. You can draw little bubbles, as in the diagram on the next page, to represent your states of mind and grade them in intensity, from positive to negative. You can also note beside the bubble any triggers that might have sent you into that mental–emotional state.

We suggest you make a bubble journal and keep it in your diary, because being "aware" is the first step to changing any negative attitudes you may have.

If you want to change into a more positive or flirtatious mood, how do you do it? We started to talk about this in chapter one. The secret is to understand that both memory and imagination use the same brain circuits we use to experience the world. This piece of technical jargon simply means your brain and body respond equally to fantasy or reality. Sports psychologists have known this for years, which is why they get top athletes to do mental rehearsal drills similar to the ones in the research with the kids shooting hoops.

Bubble journal

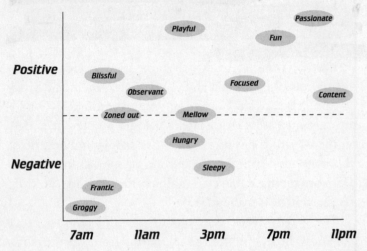

Did you see the movie *The Matrix*? When Neo was hooked up to the simulator he tried to jump between two tall buildings. He didn't make it, crashing onto the pavement instead. When they unhooked him he had blood in his mouth.

"I thought it wasn't real," he said.

"Your mind makes it real," replied Morpheus.

To get into a flirting attitude you can either remember a time when you experienced that state or imagine what it would be like to have that state. Add a pinch of mental imagery and a sound track, then turn up the feeling and you have all the ingredients needed to be playful, fun, and ready to go for it. You should practice this because you never know when you might need to just step into being flirtatious.

Mood Accessing Exercise

You might find it useful to have someone read the passage below to you a couple of times. This "snapshot" of your mood can be used at times when you need a change of attitude. It helps to repeat this exercise a few times so you know you have really got it.

Remember a time when you were chatting easily with people; a time when you felt confident and playful, even a little flirtatious. Now in your mind, fully step back into that time and re-experience it from inside your skin, looking out of your eyes.

> See what you saw, notice the smiling faces.
> Hear what you heard.
> Notice your breathing and your muscle tone.
> Feel what you felt.

Good. Now try turning up the brightness of the picture. Does that make the feeling more intense?

If it does, good; if not, try dimming the picture, or zooming in on it, or zoom out. Try adjusting the volume; does the feeling get more intense when you change the volume?

When you feel you have the most intense flirtatious attitude, take a mental snapshot of how you feel. Feels good doesn't it?

Know you can step back into this state at any time by just remembering—that's right.

Sometimes, performing a ritual will get you into the mood. Think about lighting candles for that "special" dinner. Two powerful stimuli for getting in the right mood are music and smell.

Do you have a favorite piece of music that "puts you in the mood"? Go put it on now, or play it in your head and notice how you feel.

What is your favorite scent? Obviously perfumes or aftershaves can let your brain know it's time to get flirty, but have you experimented with essential oils? If you don't know what patchouli or ylang ylang are then it's time to visit your local health food store because your brain responds powerfully to smell. In fact, when a Japanese company vaporized lemon and pumped it through their offices, the amount of data entered by their employees went up significantly.

Think of the smells that bring back memories for you, or have certain associations, or put you in the mood. Smells are very powerful when it comes to getting flirty, but perhaps not in the way you think. The scent you put on is about making *you* feel good rather than attracting a potential mate.

Guys, if you think that aftershave is going to have them flocking—think again. Some research has shown girls are more likely to be attracted by the smell of freshly baked banana bread. And as for pheromone sprays—save your money. While certain, but definitely not all, male phero-mones can cause female arousal, they are only effective at a distance of 9 or 10 feet. Unless you are up close and personal she will not have any idea where the smell is coming from, so you'll still be in competition with the other men in the room. For pheromones to have any effect you must be alone with her and if you have achieved this there are other techniques that are much more effective for arousal.

If your aftershave is not overpowering (less is more) and it makes you feel good—go for it. The better you feel about yourself the better you'll flirt.

A short word on sweat, not a guaranteed technique. Male sweat can be a turn-on to some women but only if it is fresh—so you have to time it well—if you miss your window of opportunity (20 minutes) it will *definitely* repel.

Girls, did you know your ability to smell musk, an ingredient commonly used in perfumes, is 1,000 times greater than men's? "Sexy" perfumes containing musk are therefore much more likely to arouse you when you wear them than any potential male partners. So if you like wearing perfume, do it for yourself and the way it makes you feel. If you want to have the men following you home, smell of freshly baked muffins. Seriously, research has shown that the aromas of cooking are more likely to attract and make an impact on a man.

Your Personal List

Take out your pen and notebook and answer the following to work out what gets you in a great mood.

- List three places or situations where you feel completely relaxed and at ease.
- List three places or situations that fill you with excitement or anticipation.

- What colors do you associate with feeling happy?
- What colors do you associate with flirting?
- List your three most exciting moments.
- When was the last time you knew you could do anything you set your mind to?
- List five things in your life that make you happy.
- What song makes you feel attractive and ready to flirt?
- What song gets you motivated and full of energy?
- What clothes do you wear when you are planning a day at home chilling out?
- What is your favorite outfit for flirting?
- When you want to make a good impression is there a certain outfit you wear?
- What's your favorite perfume?
- What's your favorite men's cologne?
- List your five favorite smells and what they remind you of.

Self-Talk

Something as mundane as your ritual for getting ready to go out for the evening can be a recipe for success or disaster. If you are saying to yourself, "I have nothing to wear," or "I look awful," then you are not setting yourself up to be playful and you won't go for it, will you?

In the film *Bridget Jones's Diary* there is a great scene when Bridget is getting ready to go out with her boss and is choosing which underwear to wear. Her self-talk is that if she wears the "sexy" knickers then nothing will happen.

Wanting something to happen, but not expecting that it would, Bridget doesn't wear the sexy knickers and, of course, something does happen—her boss discovers her huge panties.

Bridget uses a twisted argument with herself but the funny scene in the movie demonstrates how we all have conversations with ourselves. The style of these conversations and, in particular, the questions we ask ourselves have a powerful effect on our attitude and our ability to flirt successfully.

> *The quality of our lives is determined by the quality of the questions we ask ourselves.*
>
> Tony Robbins

Flirts ask themselves good questions, which put them in a good mood. Here are some examples of flirtatious and self-sabotaging questions.

Self-sabotaging questions	Flirtatious questions
Why don't people understand me?	What do I need to do to build rapport with people?
Why is it so hard to meet people?	What are some of the things I can do to meet more people?
Why do I find it difficult to talk to people?	What questions can I ask to get them talking about themselves?
Why can't I ever go out and just have fun?	How can I have some fun tonight?
What will I say?	How can I compliment them?
Will I look stupid?	How can I be relaxed and playful?
Am I good enough?	What do I love about people?
Is this person the one for me?	Do I like this person?

Try saying these lines to yourself and notice how they make you feel. If you catch yourself self-sabotaging, STOP and find a way to ask the question that will give you a positive feeling.

Own Your Attitude

Remember you are not your attitude or emotion, that it is just something you are feeling. Also nobody can make you think or feel anything you don't want to.

We often hear people say things like, "My partner makes me sad," "You make me so angry," or "My boss makes me feel inferior." We know that some people are very good at inviting you to feel certain emotions, but they are *your* emotions so don't let anyone lay a trip on you. Own your mood. Ultimately how you feel is up to you.

The great cartoon philosopher of our time, Charlie Brown, often demonstrated how we own our moods.

CB: "This is my sad pose."
CB: "To look sad it is important to round your shoulders and look at the ground and think sad thoughts."
CB: "If you look up, smile and think happy thoughts."
CB: "It takes all the joy out of being sad."

If you are aware you are in a blue or ugly mood, you can *stop* and realize it's your choice. Step back and choose an attitude that would be more useful. Having some pre-rehearsed triggers, such as songs, smells and memories, will make taking control of your body and brain a breeze.

You have already started to do this if you have performed the mood accessing exercise on page 21. We asked you to take a "snapshot" of when your mind and body were fully in the mood. There are ways you can make these snapshots even more memorable and intense. The secret lies in the number of circuits you've switched on in your mind and body. This is the foundation of all accelerated learning techniques. When you have decided on an attitude you want to be able to use at will, step into it, fully experience it, and then make it memorable with a word or a phrase and/or a body movement.

A friend of ours, Tim, has an amusing way of getting into his flirting attitudes. Remember the song "I'm Too Sexy" by Right Said Fred? Well, Tim does. Just before going into any situation where he has to perform he does a little dance and sings, "I'm too sexy for my shirt." You should see the change in his face and the way his body then exudes confidence.

Another friend, Amanda, has a great approach to starting each day. When she is in the shower she sings the James Brown song "I Got You (I Feel Good)" while dancing around under the water and washing her hair. By the time she's dressed and ready to face the world, she is feeling good and has put a positive spin on her day.

You'll be amazed how changing your attitude changes the way people react to you. This is because you never communicate directly with anyone; you speak with your attitude to their attitude. However, if you have bonded with someone there will be a natural tendency for him or her to shift his or her attitude to match yours.

With your intention now clear, people will be attracted to your fun, playful attitude and flirting can be a natural outcome. This is unbelievably powerful to know—by taking control of your state of mind you can subtly invite others to change their attitude and then link that "feel good" experience back to yourself.

Key Points

- You choose your moods/states of mind/attitudes.
- Flirting is a feel-good activity.
- Music and smell can alter your mood.
- Self-talk affects the way you feel and the things you do.

THREE

Marketing Yourself

To love oneself is the beginning of a lifelong romance.
Oscar Wilde, from *An Ideal Husband*

First impressions are made in seconds or fractions of seconds: marketers understand this when selling their products. When you flirt, you are marketing yourself. To do this, it's necessary to create your personal brand (how you present yourself to others) and to understand your internal marketing (how you see yourself). Then make them work in sync. This might sound impersonal but we want you to get the message and be just a bit objective about yourself for a moment.

The secret of marketing is to capture the heart and mind of the consumer, making your product desirable and memorable. When the marketing company has achieved recognition and an emotional response from consumers they have succeeded in developing a brand. When you think of Coke or Nike what do you think of? You know that Coke is "The real thing" and Nike tells you to "Just do it."

While it's important to have the consumer recognize your brand and want your product, it is equally important to have the company staffed with people who feel passionately about the company and the products. To do this, a company spends time and resources on building staff loyalty and their appreciation for the products or services the company sells. This is called internal marketing.

Whether you are in a social or business situation you are always on display, so it pays to create the right impression no matter where you are or who you are with. To do this we suggest you develop your own personal brand. As an example, Philip had come to us for coaching. He complained that whenever he saw a pretty girl he wanted to speak to he just froze. On questioning we discovered that Philip wasn't sold on his own product; he just didn't think he was good enough to speak to a pretty girl. Working with Philip we helped him to see the qualities he possessed and to realize how futile it is to self-judge because others will tend to see you as you see yourself.

Philip learned to switch off his self-judgment. He began to see meeting a girl as an opportunity to make a friend, rather than get a date. When he was out doing "field work," and branding himself as the sort of guy you would want to have as a friend, Philip spotted an attractive girl handing out leaflets at a shopping center. At first he felt his old anxiety but this time he accepted it and decided to flirt. The girl took a break to buy an ice cream and Philip wandered over and asked, "What flavor are you having?"

"It's the new Chocmint."

"Guess I'll have that too," he said.

Philip and the girl started chatting and Philip gave her a few subtle flirting signals. She told him she had noticed him while she was handing out the leaflets and hoped he would speak to her. With some encouragement from her Philip continued to flirt and she responded positively. After a few minutes the girl had to return to work but Philip got her cell phone number and sent her a text message later that day.

Developing a Sense of Self

The most important person you can flirt with is . . . yourself. How people perceive you will be determined by your own beliefs and attitudes about yourself. When we coach people we find that their ability to flirt and build relationships is improved remarkably when they see themselves in a positive, accepting way. If you feel good about yourself, flirting with someone will be easier. You can then make them feel good, so you've hit on the ultimate feel-good situation.

How well do you really understand yourself? It's time to "get naked" and take a good look. With self-knowledge you will be more comfortable reaching out to flirt with others, making them feel special while you enjoy the rewards that this brings.

If your phone is not ringing off the hook with people wanting to spend time with you then you have not yet reached "magnetic personality" status. The good news is, you are a lot closer than you think. In fact, the answer is closer than the end of your nose. Flirting can play a big part in helping you get what you want.

There's a law of nature that applies to flirting and relationships in general and that is, you have to "be" before you can "have." Many people believe they would be happy and like themselves more if they were popular or had that special person in their lives. The law of nature says you have to like yourself first.

Get Comfortable in Your Own Skin

Your attitude toward yourself is your self-esteem. Self-esteem is not the same as self-confidence; understanding the difference is important if you are going to get comfortable in your own skin.

Self-esteem is not a thing—it is a process.

Self-esteem is not fixed—it is dynamic.

The word esteem means value. Self-esteem is how we value ourselves and we are constantly valuing, judging or discounting ourselves. Negative self-talk is an example of judging or discounting: "I'll never get good at this," "I'm not good looking."

To flirt successfully, you need to stop discounting and start accepting yourself unconditionally.

Self-confidence, on the other hand, is not about who

you are. It's about what you can do. There are things you do well and things you may not have yet mastered (such as flirting). Your self-confidence is an assessment of your skills in certain areas of life.

If you have the belief "there is no failure—only feedback," then you can stop making harsh judgements about yourself. By not making judgements you leave yourself open to learning and to getting better at those things you have yet to master. When viewed in this light you can develop and build your self-confidence and your flirting skills without affecting your self-esteem.

When you like yourself and are comfortable with who you are, you will relate to other people in a more appealing way. You'll appear quietly confident rather than looking as though you are trying to get your needs met by others. There are some people, however, who just don't get the difference between confidence and arrogance. For flirting you need to get this—confidence is good, arrogance is not.

Now you may never have been to Spain and can't speak Spanish, but if you're happy to book a plane ticket, fly to Madrid, catch a taxi to a hotel and then find your way to anywhere in the city—that's self-confidence. Sure, you might get lost but you'd be resourceful and buy a map and find your way, wouldn't you?

Everybody has things they feel very confident about doing. We are guessing you feel reasonably confident you can tie your shoelaces, brush your teeth and dress yourself. There are many things you do now with confidence that you didn't always do. As our fingers fly over the keyboard working on this book we can both remember a time when neither of us felt confident turning on a computer, let alone using one to write books, balance a checkbook or bank on-line.

You might not yet feel hugely confident about going out there and flirting but you may feel really confident about who you are and the things you have already mastered. From experience you should be confident that if it can be learned you can learn it—whatever it is, it just takes information, practice and attitude. The confident approach is to say, "If someone else can do it, I can do it and I am going to have some fun learning." So take that attitude and wear it. Wear it in the way you stand, sit, breathe and walk.

To be a confident flirt and to be in the "go for it" mood, you must let go of any past hurts and rejections. If you project any of your previous baggage, it will block your flirting success.

Write the bad things that are done to you in sand, but write the good things that happen to you on a piece of marble.

Arabic proverb

Letting Go of Past Hurts Exercise
Take a piece of paper and write down any negative experiences you have had when flirting or in a relationship. Any rejections, manipulations, breaches of trust, dumpings—anything you were not happy about—write it down.

Now you can do one of two things. Take the paper and

burn it, or fold it into a paper plane to throw out of a window. Either way, use this opportunity to let go and start anew, be ready to have fun, and touch and connect with honesty, respect and understanding.

Personal Branding

Let's examine the concept of having a personal brand. The following story illustrates the power:

Five guys go to a party and see an attractive girl across the room. The first guy goes straight up to her and says, "Hi, I'm great in bed, how about it?" That's called direct marketing.

The next guy pays a friend $20 to go up to the girl and say, "Hi, my friend over there is great in bed, how about it?" That's called advertising.

The third guy gets the girl's phone number and plans to call her later to say, "I am great in bed, how about it?" That's called telemarketing.

The fourth guy starts chatting to the girl and is charming and humorous. After he gets her laughing he says, "I am great in bed, how about it?" That's called relationship marketing.

The last guy spends the early part of the evening talking to lots of different people. He is quietly confident and keeps making eye contact with the girl and smiling at her. The pretty girl walks over to *him* and says: "Hi, I'll bet you're great in bed, how about it?" That's the power of *branding*.

What we want you to explore now is how you are going to develop your personal brand. What do you want people to associate you with? Think about someone you really like or a hero from screen or television. What is it you like about them? Make a list of the things you like about them.

The following is an exercise in personal branding, so grab a pen and paper and get ready to get real. This series of questions is designed to identify your personal brand. Not every question will necessarily give you an insight, but just think about them.

1. If you were a car, what type of car would you be?
2. If you were an animal, what sort of animal would you be?
3. If you were a scent or smell, what kind of scent or smell would you be?
4. If you were a color, what color would you be?
5. If you were a food, what food would you be?

So what do they all mean? Well, there are no absolutes, but let's take a look at some possibilities.

If you consider yourself a Volvo, chances are you probably think of yourself as being "safe" or "dependable." If you describe yourself as a Porsche or Ferrari then you might be thinking you don't need a book on flirting because you are already pretty hot stuff.

The animal you choose tells a lot about the way you see yourself. We relate to these animal characteristics in our use of sayings like: as quiet as a mouse, sly like a fox, as loyal as a dog. Here is our guide to some of the more popular animals:

Animal	Characteristics
cat	balanced, wise, self-reliant
dog	devoted, loyal, trusting
bear	thoughtful, strong, need your own space
elephant	good memory, strong, family oriented
fox	cunning, adaptable, takes action
dolphin	connected to nature, gentle, aware, psychic
mouse	shy, quiet, attention to detail
lion	proud, leader, hunter (often for personal truths)
dragon	powerful, intelligent, magical

Smell is a personal, highly emotive sense. Like food, it is often tied up with memories of the past. A friend of ours likes the smell of the eau de cologne 4711, which her grandmother wore. Although it is not a popular scent today, she loves it and often chooses perfumes that contain neroli, the predominant scent in 4711. Similarly some people love the smell of Old Spice, an aftershave that was popular in the 1960s. It's the associations, the pleasant memories, that often draw us to a smell or a taste.

When you are choosing what smells or food you would be, take some time to think what memory it is that attracts you to it. This will give you some insight into what motivates your choice.

Our responses to color are subjective and are often culturally based. While some responses are widely known and accepted, not all cultures are in agreement. For instance, to the Irish, green is the mythical color of fairies, leprechauns and the magical shamrock, whereas to Muslims, green has religious significance and is thought to have been the color favored by Muhammed (it is also the color of the holy flag that was carried into battle when Mecca was conquered). Similarly, in Western tradition white is the color for brides and signifies optimism and peace, whereas in traditional Asian societies it signifies mourning and would never be worn at a wedding or celebration.

Beyond these broader cultural associations, it is believed that our favorite colors reveal something about our personal qualities. We've identified some of the more common associations in the table below.

Color	Qualities
white	optimistic, peaceful, gentle, high standards for self and others, critical
blue	calm, relaxed, secure, confident, independent, responsible, judgmental
yellow	stimulating, happy, intelligent, optimistic, organized, bossy
orange	happy, good self-esteem, forgiving, good humored, friendly, impatient
red	powerful, assertive, determined, warm, sensual, angry
green	harmonious, relaxed, prosperous, connected to nature, tendency to be irresponsible
violet	calm, artistic, intuitive, spiritual, sensitive, compassionate, vulnerable
black	mysterious, dramatic, self-controlled, authoritarian, strong-willed, disciplined

The next exercise reveals how you perceive yourself. If you want to know how your personal brand will be perceived in the marketplace, take these questions to a trusted friend. Ask them to answer them in relation to how they see you. Their answers might surprise you—but they'll be incredibly valuable. You'll get a good idea of how others see you and as feedback is the breakfast of champions, eat up. Once you feel game, ask for a second helping.

Me Brand

With some newfound self-awareness and extra knowledge of how others perceive you, it's time for you to come up with your "Me Brand." Write down your personal profile—make it at least fifty words long. Some suggestions of what to describe include:

- who you are—not what you do
- your positive attributes
- what you care about
- what you have contributed to
- your dreams and aspirations.

You may be surprised, having done this exercise, how much clearer you are about who you are and what you have to offer, as well as how your future interactions can be more natural and fun.

Being clearer about who you are frees you to experience the individuality of those you flirt with. You'll care less about what they may think of you and more about what they think of themselves, allowing you to build a bridge by talking about their favorite topic—themselves.

Getting Noticed

> *It's better to be looked over than overlooked.*
>
> Mae West

So why do you need to get noticed?

If you can get someone to notice you, more than 50 percent of the work is done. To be noticed you only need to capture someone's attention for a few seconds. Once they become aware of you, it's up to you to take some steps to be sure you make a good impression.

Sam was applying for a job at an advertising agency. The job was in the mailroom, but Sam knew this was where he had to start if he wanted a career in advertising. The agency advertised this position at the same time each year. Their policy was to either promote or terminate the mailroom staff at the end of a year at the job, depending on the employees' performance.

Sam knew he would be one of hundreds of applicants and he wanted to be noticed so he needed to set himself apart from all the others. He spent a week on his application and, with the help of a graphic artist, came up with a professionally styled and presented application in the form of an advertisement about himself, telling the agency what the advantages of employing him would be. He got an interview first and then the job, and had moved on from the mailroom within six months of joining the agency. From day one the management had him tagged as someone special.

Posture

In chapter two we mentioned Charlie Brown's sad posture. When you enter a social situation do you move and stand in a confident way or do you have a sad posture? Do you look as though you are enjoying yourself, ready to have fun, or does your posture scream shyness or stress? How you think affects your posture and your posture affects how you think. The mind and body are inextricably linked.

When we are coaching or doing our workshops we have a lot of fun playing around with posture. Remember the mood accessing exercise? You can use this to feel playful, confident, alive and flirtatious. Just by thinking the thoughts and remembering how it feels you can be confident, elegant and playful, and you can go for it. And if you can't remember ever feeling like this, imagine what it would be like while you adopt the posture of these emotions.

The secret to getting noticed is to carry yourself in such a way that people notice how you move. Do you remember seeing someone move through a room looking cool? How did it feel to watch them? What were your impressions? Now think about someone lumbering through that same space awkwardly. Sense the difference you feel as an observer.

Ever notice how some people just seem to know how to sit comfortably and appear calm and composed when doing so? Compare this with the person who sits looking like a sack of potatoes thrown into a corner. Again, the difference between these people is in their posture. It's a fact that we make judgements about people and they make judgements about us in a split second. Don't underestimate how important your posture is to your success in relationships.

Good posture is about getting your mind connected with your body so you notice how you feel. Yoga and Pilates classes are great for getting connected to your body and mind in this way. They are also very "in" at the moment, so there'll be plenty of opportunities for you to meet people and practice your flirting at the same time.

Standing Roll-down Exercise

This is the first move of a Pilates class. Because it can make a significant impact on your mind–body connection it can make you a much more powerful flirt.

Wearing comfortable loose-fitting clothes, stand barefooted on a flat surface. Make sure your weight is evenly distributed between each foot and ensure each foot has three points of contact with the floor—the ball of the foot, the base of the little toe and the heel. These are your tripods.

Imagine a line joining the two bony points at the front of your pelvis. This is called your "B line." It should be closer to your spine than your navel—to achieve this, gently contract your pelvic floor muscles so your "B line" is drawn toward your spine. You should be able to do this and still be able to breathe comfortably.

Now imagine your shoulder-blades being drawn downward toward your back pockets.

Feel your head being pulled upward toward the sky or ceiling.

Breathe deeply and fully.

As you exhale by sighing, roll your head forward, then

your shoulders. Roll your spine forward so that your hands move toward the floor. If the backs of your legs feel tight, allow your knees to bend slightly.

At the end of the sigh you should be fully bent forward at the hips.

Stay there as you inhale fully, imagining you are breathing in through your armpits.

As you exhale again, draw in your "B line" and roll your spine up, vertebra by vertebra, like a string of beads being rolled up against an imaginary wall.

When you are back standing on your tripods, draw in your "B line" again, draw your shoulder-blades back, extend your head to the ceiling, breathe in and repeat the roll forward.

Do this seven to ten times every morning and you'll be surprised how flexible and centered you feel.

Dress

There is a great story about how Sophia Loren got her first break in movies. She managed to get an invite to a party where she knew there would be many producers and directors. It was a swanky affair and all the women were dressed to the nines, complete with expensive jewelry. Wanting to be noticed, Sophia chose a simple white cotton dress and wore no jewelry. Every man in the room noticed her. The rest is history.

This one's for the girls. Most guys enjoy a little mystery. A flash of thigh or a hint of shoulder is enough to let his imagination run wild. Keep in mind that the less you show, the more he will have to fantasize about.

And for the guys, girls spend a whole lot of time thinking about what they are going to wear and preparing to look their best. They appreciate a guy who has given some thought to his appearance and his clothing too. Understated and stylish will always get you noticed for your good taste. When you put some effort into your clothing, you'll stand out from the crowd.

History's greatest flirt, Casanova, had an extensive wardrobe and knew how to use it for maximum effect. Casanova's fellow countrymen have continued to understand the importance of style when it comes to impressing the opposite sex. In fact, Italians spend twice the percentage of their disposable income on clothes than the citizens of any other nation in the world.

Even if you prefer hanging around in an old T-shirt and jeans, you're going to need something a bit more impressive in your wardrobe. Luckily for you, among your family, friends or acquaintances there is bound to be a woman who enjoys dressing men. Enlist her help in going through your wardrobe and getting rid of the ratty stuff. Once your wardrobe is rid of the rat, let her take you shopping and listen to her suggestions.

Where dress is concerned, the most important thing to remember is to feel comfortable and dress for the occasion.

Key Points

- Create the right impression.
- You have to "be" before you can "have."

- Let go of baggage from your past.
- Develop a personal brand.
- Get comfortable in your own skin.
- Adopt good posture.
- Dress well.

FOUR

Choosing When . . .

The doors we open and close each day decide the lives we live.

Flora Whittemore

Knowing the right time, right place and right situation to flirt is second nature to most great flirts. As we said in chapter one, "because true flirting is ambiguous you can always get away with it anywhere." So why are we discussing choosing when and where to flirt? Although you can flirt anywhere, there are times and places where it's wiser to rein in your flirting and other times where, if you are not in tune with what's going on around you, you'll miss great flirting opportunities.

Take the story of 19-year-old John and his buddies catching a cab home from a disappointing night at a local club. The cab driver asked them if they had had a good night. The guys grumbled that it was okay. "Didn't you score?" asked the cab driver. John and his friends hadn't.

"You know," said the cabbie, "I just picked up two carloads of pretty girls from that place, and they were all complaining that not one guy even bothered to say hello to them."

John and his buddies learned a lesson that night. While his friends shrugged it off, John never made that mistake again. He has gone on to be a great flirt because he now always makes a point of making contact with people by smiling and saying hello.

Making Contact

There are two initial ways of making contact with someone. The first is making eye contact. If there is any interest, eye contact is most often followed by the second, smiling. These are two simple and risk-free ways of starting to flirt.

Making eye contact is simple. It's *briefly* looking over in someone's direction and catching their eye. You can do this from across a crowded room or as you are making your way over to introduce yourself. Often two people will make eye contact a number of times before one or the other makes the initial approach. But don't confuse making eye contact with staring. Staring at someone until they look in your direction is not a good move. If you stare at someone it will likely make them think you are some kind of creepy psychopath or a potential stalker.

Once you are deep in conversation with someone, make eye contact regularly and hold their gaze for just a few seconds longer than usual. This has a real impact. Any longer than a few extra seconds and you'll risk weirding them out.

You'll learn a lot about your companion from making eye contact. Trust your intuition here. Whatever you feel from looking in their eyes will give you a good indication of how things are progressing.

For the women, if you want your eye contact to have an effect, remember men love to be heroes. Even in this modern age their favorite fantasy is slaying dragons. So think medieval demure damsel and look at him from beneath your upper lashes with your head slightly up-turned toward him. If you are the same height as the man, at his eye level, find a seat to display your adoration. Don't flash him a seductive smoldering gaze; that's moved on from flirting to seduction and he'll read you as being a predator. If he senses you are a predator he will either back off and lose interest or think you have given him the green light to rip your clothes off as soon as you are alone. Of course, if that's what you're after . . .

For the guys, look her in the eyes and not at her cleavage. Genuine interest in what she is saying and her point of view will win you her heart almost as fast as a leery long look at her breasts will get you a withering stare and her hasty departure. She loves a man who is interested in what she thinks and how she feels. The best way for you to acknowledge her is to make eye contact when she is saying something she feels passionate about and gently nod in agreement. She will take this as a compliment as well as an acknowledgment that you are hearing what she is saying.

Eye contact before and during flirting makes the experience more intense and communicates emotions and feelings between you. Make regular eye contact for as long as you want the flirting to continue. It hooks the other person into the moment and into you. Practice making eye contact with strangers in a safe place, such as a coffee shop or supermarket.

Research has shown that a plain person who smiles is more attractive to the opposite sex than an attractive person who doesn't smile. It doesn't matter how drop-dead gorgeous you are, nobody is going to come near you if you don't know how to smile. It's now time to work on an award-winning smile.

We think of people who smile as being happy, cheerful, friendly, confident and fun loving. When you smile at someone, it is the ultimate acknowledgment. It says, "I've noticed you and noticing you makes me smile." What sort of message does that send? Think about it. How do you feel when people smile at you? What do you think when you see someone smile? Smiling is infectious to all but the most grumpy of people and, frankly, we don't want to flirt with them, do we?

How potent is it to smile at a stranger? Try it and see. Smiling can send a whole lot of different messages. It all depends on the emotional intent of your smile. Go on, practice smiling at everyone you make eye contact with for the next 24 hours. You'll see from their responses to you what message they're getting.

We are not suggesting you walk around with a freeze-frame smile stuck on your face. We are talking about developing the biggest, brightest, flash your teeth, genuine smile you can muster.

When you smile at someone you find attractive the message that will be sent is just that—they are attractive. Guys, if you leer at someone they'll get that message loud and clear and you might be on the receiving end of a disdainful glare instead of a smile. Girls, the same goes for you too. The guys like a smile to show you appreciate them, not that you are sizing them up—send the right message. This has everything to do with sending clear messages.

If you don't smile readily then you are going to have to start practicing until your face aches. If that made you laugh, you might not realize how serious smiling is. Go on—think about it. How approachable is someone who is always brooding, moody and glum? Now think about a person who always has a ready smile for you. Learn to smile and love it.

If you need to, practice in front of a mirror. Don't just smile—imagine you have spotted your best buddy, someone you haven't seen for ages. How would that make you feel? What would your smile be like for them? Think of that awesome guy or girl you want to meet. They are coming toward you, looking and smiling at you. Smile back at them and feel what it feels like. Think of one of the happiest times in your life. Go back there in your mind and feel the happiness all over again.

Does a smile come readily to you? What does it feel like? Now you are getting the hang of what it takes to practice smiling for your flirt toolbox. Go out there and smile at everybody you make eye contact with.

Risk Taking and Rejection

In the last chapter we asked you to undertake a "letting go of past hurts" exercise and get into a "go for it" attitude. If you are hanging onto any past baggage you are likely to carry it into any new connections or relationships, and that can really hold you back.

Having the right go-for-it attitude allows you to flirt with anybody and to observe their response. If it doesn't work out you will not take it personally. You know that there is no such thing as failure in flirting, just feedback. You can always learn something every time you flirt, even if that something is "don't ever do that again!"

Whenever we connect or attempt to connect with someone, there is always a risk. The risk can be that the connection doesn't happen or that it goes too far. Sometimes your flirting can be misconstrued. Instead of just enjoying the fun, the person you are flirting with takes a mental leap and thinks you are romantically interested. The question is what do you do when someone gets the wrong idea.

Of course an ounce of prevention is better than a pound of cure, so it is always better to speak up sooner rather than later. "We are just having fun aren't we?" is a good question to pose if you suspect your flirting is being taken too seriously. Consider the following scenarios, as you might find some good tips on what else you can do.

Maria was having a party at her place and was enjoying herself immensely. She was dancing with Ben, who had been brought along by a friend. Ben was a good dancer and so Maria was taking advantage of the chance to dance with a guy who knew his left foot from his right. Suddenly it struck Maria that Ben was reading more into the dancing than she was. Since many think dancing is "the vertical expression of a horizontal desire," this is not an unusual situation. Maria looked Ben straight in the eye and delivered the question in a cool and assertive way. Ben gulped, but received the message loud and clear—the dancing was just about having fun now and not a prelude to sex. By calling the score early in the piece Maria avoided fending off a drunken grope later in the evening.

Chris pays attention to the slightest details. He met Sasha at a book launch and they found themselves teasing each other over their choice of reading material. Chris and Sasha swapped business cards and agreed to catch up again, which they did a few weeks later. At the coffee shop they again found they enjoyed each other's company and there was a definite chemistry between them. After the coffee Chris sent Sasha a text message letting her know how much he had enjoyed their time together. There followed a series of to and fro flirtatious text messages, resulting in catching up for drinks later in the week. At a trendy city bar, Chris and Sasha started to play the twenty questions game—you ask a question, I ask a question. Chris discovered Sasha had only just separated from her husband and was still dealing with some issues. Chris was sensitive enough to realize Sasha was not yet ready for a new relationship, so he said to her, "I get the feeling what you really need right now is a friend, not a lover." Sasha was relieved. She enjoyed Chris's company but she knew he was right. She was not yet ready to start a new relationship.

Chris and Sasha are still good friends and still flirt with each other on the understanding that they are both just having fun. This would have been unlikely if Chris hadn't been clear about his intentions early on to keep the flirting and the friendship on a "for fun" only basis.

Great flirting creates an energy flow that is playful, fun and engaging but never over the top, slutty or over-enthusiastic. Good flirts don't appear to be trying hard to impress, they are never pushy, annoying or loud. If you get over-confident when you are flirting, you could find yourself performing *for* an audience rather than flirting *with* someone. If this happens you have shifted your attention from the person you are flirting with to yourself.

As you develop your flirting skills you'll understand the impact of being subtle. You don't ever need to over-play your flirting. Remember, when the flirting goes from ambiguous to obvious you're crossing the line and you're into seduction.

Business and Workplace Flirting

Flirting is useful in business. It can smooth over some rough patches and it can make your journey through the corporate jungle a lot more enjoyable. It can also bring you face to face with the people who need to know who you are.

Good salespeople flirt with gatekeeping receptionists and PAs to get past them to the decision makers. Keeping the flirting fun, playful and light-hearted can mean the difference between success and disaster. As a skilled flirt you'll be able to lighten up any situation in the workplace. When you flirt with someone you pay them a compliment and compliments can grease the wheels of industry.

The workplace is definitely a place where you must remember that less is more and keep your flirting subtle. At work stay away from any suggestive remarks that go beyond flirting unless you get a lot of very clear green-light signals from the other person. There are boundaries. In terms of sexual harassment in the workplace, no employee has to put up with lewd comments, invasion of personal space and touching as part of a day at work. However, if you are afraid to pay a compliment or have a little fun then work becomes boring and unproductive. A happy balance is easily found by remembering the intention of flirting is to make the other person feel good. To apply this rule to your communications ask yourself, "Will this make them feel good?" You can't go wrong if the answer is yes.

It's easy to figure out that if you are going to be successful in the corporate world you need to get along with people, and certain people are the key to helping you achieve what you want. By flirting with these key people your business life will blossom. Who is it that makes your day go smoother? Is it your secretary, the person in the mailroom, your boss, your client? Have you set an intention to make them feel good and like you? What can you do? The simple answer is everything we share in this book.

Notice them, step into their shoes, pay them a compliment, be a little mischievous—but remember, work is *the* place where you cross the line at your peril.

Where to Flirt?

As you begin to understand the flirting skills, you'll want to practice them. The question then arises, "But where?" Almost everywhere! Flirting makes you and the other person feel good why would you not use it generously? Here are a few ideas to get you going.

Public Transportation

The inevitability of standing or being seated next to strangers means you have an almost inexhaustible supply of people to flirt with. For example, whenever Michael takes the train to and from school, he never misses a chance to flirt. At the time of writing, Michael had met two girls by just saying "hi" on the train.

Workshops

Have you been to your public library or community center lately? Somewhere around reception there is probably an information board bursting with brochures on every type of course imaginable, from yoga to basket weaving. Latin dancing is popular at the moment, or you might be more interested in film appreciation. Whatever your taste, workshops are a great way to meet like-minded people and you can take these opportunities to flirt with them.

Coffee Shops

Coffee shops are the temples of people-watching and what better way to practice your non-verbal rapport skills than when sipping a latte? As with public transportation there is often a shortage of seats, so this lends itself to the opportunity to say, "Excuse me, may I share your table? . . . Thank you, by the way my name is . . ."

Retail Therapy

Shop salespeople are often willing to engage in a flirtatious exchange. They can be bored by a lack of customers or they might be used to customers being short with them or in a rush. Pick a time when the assistant is not too busy and have some fun. Guys, you could try a ladies' fashion store and tell the assistant you are shopping for your sister. Girls, go to a hi-tech outlet and have fun pretending to know how to make a floppy become a hard drive (*see* chapter seven for double entendres).

Singles' Nights

Check out your local paper for singles' nights. Yes, we know they can be a bit of a meat market but if you go with the intention of using the evening to practice your skills then you can actually end up having a lot of fun.

Christina, a beautiful but shy girl, told us that she recently went to a large singles' gathering with the intention of just saying "hello" to ten men. It didn't count if they first said "hello" to her. When her mission was accomplished she left . . . with her self-confidence so much higher than when she arrived.

Off-Beat Ideas

In the movie *About a Boy* the character played by Hugh Grant pretends to have a son so he can hang out at single parents' meetings in the hope of picking up a single mom.

Then there was the caller we heard on a local radio station who went to weight-loss meetings because he thought the women there would be easier to chat up and more likely to agree to go out with him.

We know you can do better. When you do, send us an e-mail and tell us about how and where you flirted, and what happened. We look forward to hearing your stories.

Key Points

- Right time, right action, right place—timing is everything.
- Great flirts know when to flirt and when not to flirt.
- Make eye contact.
- Smile, smile, smile.
- Set boundaries and take notice of other people's boundaries.
- Flirting for business can open doors and make the workplace more fun.

FIVE

Get in Step

*Everyone is kneaded out of the same dough but
not baked in the same oven.*

Yiddish proverb

Have you ever had the experience where you just
"clicked" with someone? You may have just met them
but you immediately felt comfortable, sort of in-tune, as
if you have known them for ages. More often than not
this is what is known as serendipity. What if you knew
the secret to creating this instant connection?

One of the most powerful flirting tools is the ability to build rapport, to get in step with someone else. Being able to instantly create a relationship of trust and emotional connection is what flirting is all about.

To get in step easily you will need the flirting attitudes of taking notice and loving people. The taking-notice attitude is when you can look at someone and really observe them without any judgment. When you do this you will find yourself naturally getting in step. There are a number of components to getting in step:

- physically mirroring
- communicating in the same style
- verbally matching their interests.

Physically Mirroring

Have you ever watched two people in a restaurant who were obviously in love? How did you know they were? Was it the way their bodies were a perfect mirror of each other? This is the most obvious sign that two people share rapport.

Another example is two good buddies standing chatting at a bar. If one has his left leg forward, the other will have his right leg forward. If one has his right elbow on the bar the other will have his left.

Mirroring is easy because it is natural to do. You simply adopt the same posture as the other person, starting with the head, then the body, then the arms and legs. If you really want to make a connection, change your breathing to the same depth and frequency as theirs.

Mirroring Exercise

Enlist a friend and ask them to sit and talk to you for five minutes about something they are interested in or their last vacation. As they talk, consciously notice and copy how they hold their head, their body posture, and where they place their arms and their legs. When you have become a mirror of their body, notice where they are breathing. Is it in the upper, middle or lower chest? How fast is it? Now do the same.

Become really present, be in the moment, listening and interested in everything your friend says. Do this without judgment, accepting everything they say as if it is the most important information you have ever heard.

If your friend changes posture or moves during the exercise, count silently to five and adjust your posture to mirror them again.

After five minutes, stop and ask your friend how it felt to be mirrored by you. Chances are it felt good. If you want to find out what happens without rapport, repeat the exercise but deliberately let your attention wander and avoid mirroring them. Instead choose different gestures and posture. You'll notice they will find it hard to talk without stumbling and will unconsciously try to get your attention or just give up.

Sometimes it is not appropriate to directly mirror someone, so a more subtle approach is to match them. An example of matching would be if someone crosses their arms, you cross your legs. If they are tapping a pen, you tap your foot at the same rate.

One way to observe the power of this technique is when you are sitting in a bar or café. You will notice someone doing something rhythmic like the preceding example, so match the beat with another part of your body. Watch the person out of the corner of your eye and you'll observe them becoming aware of you. How cool is that?

Developing an acute awareness of non-verbal cues, such as breathing and body posture, will allow you to get feedback as to how you are doing. Do they like you? Is your message being received? Do you need to change the way you are communicating?

Later in this book you will learn the twenty-one non-verbal signals specific to flirting.

Communicating in the Same Style

People have different preferences for receiving information and different styles for sharing it. Did you ever have a TV that had a "rabbit ears" antenna? Remember how you had to move those rabbit ears around to get a good signal? A great flirt tunes into the signal the other person is broadcasting—this is communicating.

There are three broad preferred styles of communication to be aware of:

- lookers
- listeners
- feelers.

The Lookers

Alternatively known as visual people, lookers process information as pictures. Everybody does this to a certain extent but these people do it more and do it more intensely. You can spot a visual by their eye movements, their speech and their clothes. Lookers have a continual stream of pictures running inside their mind and you can observe them repeatedly looking up as they talk to view or access these pictures.

As we all know light travels very fast and this is often the speed at which lookers speak. They talk fast and often in high tones, get bored easily and often change the subject. If you are not a visual type, strap yourself in and go for a ride. Another sure sign you are flirting with a visual person is their dress sense—bright and colorful is a must as they are very particular about appearance. Words used by lookers are descriptive and relate to the pictures they are making in their head. Examples of these are:

- I see what you mean
- that seems clear
- can you show me?

When communicating with a looker it is important to approximate their speed, tone and manner of speech.

The Listeners

Called auditory, listeners are attuned to sound. For them, more so than others, it is not just what you say but how you say it. Listeners speak slower than lookers and if you listen you'll hear more rhythm or variation in their tone. Most radio announcers have a strong auditory preference as they only have the one channel to communicate with—sound.

You'll notice that listeners breathe more in the mid chest and this can make them appear more solid in the torso than the visuals, who breathe fast in the upper chest. When you watch someone with a strong auditory preference you'll see their eyes move from side to side as they process information. Listeners like to use language and often have an extensive vocabulary. You'll hear them use phrases such as:

- that sounds right
- rings a bell
- I'm in tune with what you are saying
- tell me about it.

To bond with listeners get in tune and reply with rhythm.

The Feelers

These people are called feelers because they are in touch with their feelings. This not to say that lookers and listeners aren't; but feelers have to take information and run it through their body as well as their mind. This process takes a little time so feelers, or kinaesthetics, will speak more slowly than the other two communicating styles. Feelers breathe slow and deep and you can observe their eyes look down as they "go inside" to think and feel.

Feelers want to:

- get a handle on things
- wrap my mind around it
- get in touch with what's important
- walk through the process.

If you want to bond with a feeler and this is not your natural style, slow down. The trick is to move your breathing to your belly; when you do this you'll find that it is a lot easier to pace. Often feelers use more gestures than the other styles, so you can copy these too.

It's useful to watch someone's eyes when you are speaking to them. The eyes are hard-wired to the brain and they move depending on whether the person is making pictures in their head, focusing on sounds or getting in touch with how they feel.

Are You a Looker, a Listener or a Feeler?

Rapport building is fun to learn. Practice these exercises and you'll really get a feel for building rapport. Circle all the responses that apply to you.

1. What attracts me to others is
   a. how they look
   b. how they sound
   c. how they move

2. When I am talking to someone, I
   a. see what they are saying
   b. hear what they are saying
   c. get a feeling for what they mean

3. When I am lost, I
   a. refer to a map
   b. ask for directions
   c. trust my gut instinct

4. I prefer to
   a. go to the movies, watch TV or a video
   b. go to a concert, listen to music or the radio
   c. play a sport or do something physical

5. When I have lots of things to do, I
   a. make a list or imagine myself doing them
   b. keep reminding myself to do them
   c. feel uneasy until they are done

6. I prefer books or magazines
   a. with lots of pictures
   b. with great articles
   c. which are practical and how to

7. I go to places where
   a. I can watch people
   b. there is music, conversation or quiet
   c. there are things to do

8. If I have a problem, I
   a. look for ways to solve it
   b. talk about solutions
   c. churn it over until it feels right

9. When learning something new, it is easier for me to
   a. have someone show me how to do it
   b. have someone explain what to do
   c. get in and do it myself

Count up the number of a, b and c responses.

Totals: a (looker) _____ b (listener) _____ c (feeler) _____

Now make a bar graph of your scores. Here is an example of one of ours.

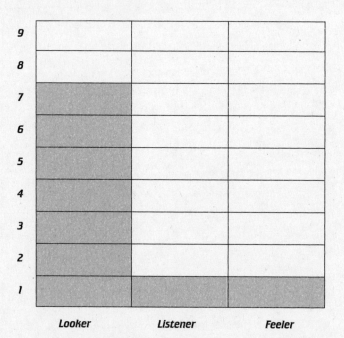

Having done this exercise, it should be obvious what your communication preference is. You'll find it easier to flirt with people with a similar preference. Knowing what you do now, you can develop a flexibility to flirt with those who have a different preference.

Communication is not what you say but what the other person hears. Rapport is when you use all channels of communication, including body language, breathing, facial expressions and voice, to match the other person's communication preference so your message is clearly received, understood and accepted.

As you master flirting you will become more aware and adept at tuning in *with* other people because you will be able to adapt your style to "click" with everyone you want to. Language is your way of communicating your thoughts and experiences. Good flirts are good listeners.

Verbally Matching Their Interests

It's irresistible when you meet someone who shows a genuine interest in you and wants to know about your thoughts and opinions on a whole range of topics. It's hard not to be drawn to someone who really listens to you and encourages you to talk about yourself.

Emily, a client of ours, meets lots of people in her job at a private hospital and through an active social life. She is a great socializer who loves to chat but is frustrated at how often people talk about themselves and never seem interested in each other. It's like the line from Bette Midler in the movie *Beaches*, when after a long monologue she says, "That's enough about me, what about you? What do you think about me?"

Emily was naturally a good listener, which meant that this was the role she found herself in a lot of the time. At a work-related seminar she had the chance to meet and interact with people in the same industry from all over the country. Most of these people she had not met before and she looked forward to exchanging ideas and making some new contacts.

On the first day of the seminar she was seated next to Jess. Like Emily, Jess was chatty and friendly and the two were happily talking within a minute of sitting down.

Emily and Jess spent the entire day together during the seminar as well as during coffee breaks and lunch. At the end of the day Emily suggested they meet before the seminar the next morning for breakfast.

Emily arrived home and mentioned to her boyfriend what a great day it had been, and that she had made a new friend, someone she had lots in common with. When Emily's boyfriend asked about her new friend, Emily was surprised to realize she knew almost nothing about Jess. Although the two women had spent most of their time together Jess had spent the day asking Emily about herself. Unused to this role, and seduced by the enjoyment of it, Emily had talked about herself, her work, her opinions. Yet Emily's most vivid recollection of the day had been what a great person Jess was.

When you are flirting remember that people love to talk about themselves and tell their stories. For example, you come back from a sensational vacation and someone asks you, "How was your trip?" Before you get past the part about arriving at the hotel, they interrupt you with, "Oh when we went there a few years ago . . ." and then proceed to tell the story of their trip while you sit in open-mouthed silence. As we said, people love to talk about themselves.

If you are flirting to impress and you ask a question, let the other person finish answering, and consider what they said before you launch into your own response. Even then, be careful not to make the other person's story or point sound trivial against your own. Remember, a great flirt likes to ask open-ended questions that require more than a yes or no answer.

Learning to be a good listener is an essential part of being a good flirt, whether it is a first date or coffee with a work mate. Make it your habit to engage the other person and show genuine interest in what they are saying. This habit carries with it a bonus beyond the flattering appearance of your interest. The person opposite you is providing a flowing river of information into which you can cast your line and hook out many good flirting opportunities.

Learn how to listen and see things from another person's point of view and discover what is important to them. By doing this you can create a deep connection with that person. It has been said you can't really know a man until you have walked a mile in his shoes. Even if you can't take a walk in someone else's shoes, you can at least step into them. And even if you find they don't fit too well, you'll at least know a little bit more about the person and will be able to make a stronger bond with them.

Some people are naturally empathetic and concern themselves with the feelings and viewpoints of others. This makes them great people-persons. These people generally have lots of friends because others like spending time with them and feel good in their company. Empathetic people do need to set some boundaries. Without boundaries they run the risk of others taking advantage of their selflessness.

Then there are people who are incredibly self-centred and oblivious to or simply don't care about the feelings or viewpoints of others. Being self-centred is not characteristic of the flirting attitude; you need to focus on the other person rather than on yourself. In flirting your rewards come after you have made someone else feel good.

Changing Places

This exercise is designed to develop your empathy and understanding of other people while maintaining boundaries. These are skills that will prove very useful in flirting as well as in friendships and business dealings.

You can do this exercise alone or with a friend. You'll need three chairs, two facing each other and one off to one side.

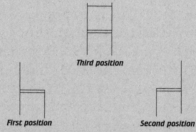

Third position

First position   **Second position**

Sit in one of the chairs facing each other (the first position) and have your partner sit opposite (second position). If you are doing this alone imagine someone you know well sitting in second position.

When you are in first position you see the person in second position through your eyes. You experience them through your senses. You evaluate them through your filters. This is the self-centred way of relating to someone. If you were in second position you would see what they see, feel what they feel, and so on.

Your mind has the flexibility to conceive what it would be like to be in the second position. You can imagine what it would be like to "be" that person—how they feel, how they see the world. Try this for a few moments and you'll be amazed at the insights you get. For added effect you can get up from your chair and move to the other chair and imagine "stepping in" to the other person's attitude. We know it sounds weird, but try it and see.

In day-to-day conversations it is not always easy or desirable to shift to the second position; however, you can move your awareness to the third position, the chair off to the side. In this position you will be aware of yourself and your communication style as well as the other person. You can therefore take their feelings into account too. You can see both yourself and the other person at the same time. When you try the third position notice how your awareness changes. This third position's attitude has a similar feel to the "peripheral vision" exercise you will do in chapter five. The more you do this, the more you'll find yourself combining the two techniques. You'll be surprised how much you pick up about someone and how connected they feel to you.

People like to talk about their interests, beliefs and values. By encouraging them to talk about what is important to them and actively listening, you'll be able to flirt in a way that shows you have not only listened to them but you have heard and understood what they said. The greatest compliment you can pay anyone is to really "get" them.

It's been said that babies cry for it and men will die for it. What is *it*? Recognition.

By listening with all your senses you are recognizing a person. When you flirt and create a connection, people will open up to you. Once you get past the superficial and mundane topics, such as "Gee, isn't it busy in here?" or

"How's the weather been lately?" you'll start to uncover the person's beliefs and values. Beliefs and values are the mind stuff that makes us who we are.

Your beliefs are thoughts or ideas you have confirmed to yourself over time. Most of your beliefs you would have picked up between the ages of two and seven, yet they continue to drive the behaviors you have today. This is why getting to know yourself is important.

We all need to change beliefs about the world and ourselves when we don't find them useful. For instance, you might not have believed you are a great flirt but now that you are coming to realize how much fun it is, you'll be willing to give it a go.

It is important to remember not to challenge a person's beliefs when flirting. People are emotional about strongly held beliefs. The great flirter will show a deep interest in those beliefs and how they drive the other person's behavior. This is because a flirt is a student of human nature, always curious about what makes people tick.

Your values are what excite you, inspire you and make you feel connected to who you are. What you value attracts you and motivates you. The great flirt knows that to get in step they need to:

- say nothing while the other person is speaking—don't interrupt
- pause before responding—it lets the other person know they have been heard
- use the exact words and phrases the person has used back to them
- get the spirit of what is being said or get confirmation by saying, "Let me make sure I understand you . . ."

Reflect back to the other person by using comments such as "Let me get the picture . . ." or "It sounds like . . ." or "I get the feeling . . ."—the different types of responses by lookers, listeners and feelers. Prompt the person to say more or direct the conversation by making comments such as "Really, tell me more" or "I want to hear more about . . . ."

Key Points

- Get in step and build rapport.
- Find out if you are a looker, listener or feeler.
- Find out if the other person is a looker, listener or feeler.
- Show interest in the other person.
- Don't talk too much about yourself.
- See things from the other person's viewpoint.

SIX

Insight

> *The most important thing in communication is to hear what isn't being said.*
>
> Peter F. Drucker

Since time began and creatures walked, crawled, climbed or slithered upon this earth, members of the animal kingdom have courted and flirted using body language. The purpose of flirting for animals was to find a mate and populate. We, however, have the pleasure of flirting for the fun of it, without it having to lead to anything more than sharing a few laughs and a whole lot of good feelings.

Body language, or non-verbal communication, is a powerful force in the flirting game because it is, more often than not, unconscious. We are in constant communication with each other—our bodies are speaking even when we're not, so it's important to be aware of what messages we're sending. Great flirts take notice of the body language and signals that people send.

How often do you find yourself running a hand through your hair while talking to someone? Next time you do, check your feelings; chances are there is someone close by who has sparked your interest. Guys often tilt their heads back slightly and run a casual hand through their hair. Look to see what direction their head is tilting and you'll be likely to see the object of their interest. If it's tilted toward a mirror, move on.

Girls have a whole lot of hair moves. They run a hand through their hair, twirl it around their fingers, flip it and even spend time inspecting the state of their hair by pulling it close to their faces. Trouble is, while most of these preening moves are a sign of interest, some can be a sign of boredom. We'll talk about signals later on in more detail.

Playing with your clothes is another way of drawing attention to yourself but, again, the signals may get lost in the translation. A woman adjusting her clothes is often taken as a sign of interest; however, it can also be an indication that she is feeling self-conscious or ill at ease. Of course, if she climbs up on a stool, crosses her legs and lifts the hem of her skirt ever so slightly then it's almost a sure bet that she finds you attractive. The guy equivalent of this is pushing or rolling his sleeves up if he is wearing a long-sleeved shirt. If he loosens his tie at the same time then you know you're making him hot.

Starting with Desmond Morris's *The Naked Ape*, reams have been written about body language. Our aim here is not to rehash what has already been well covered, instead we are going to concentrate on the body language and signals that relate to flirting. We'll alert you to things you can watch for and techniques you can play with to find out who is in the mood to flirt. We'll tell you how to read body language messages and how to send them. You'll be amazed at how much richer your communication will be when you tap into this non-verbal channel. It's like going from a small TV screen to a plasma screen.

Peripheral Vision Exercise

Something worth developing in observing non-verbals is your peripheral vision. We have two ways of looking at things, focused (up close) and wide angle. When you let your focus relax you can take in much more information. This also allows you to watch without staring.

Focus your eyes on a point about 10 feet up on a wall, about 16 feet away from you. Continue to see that point but increase your awareness of what's around it. Gradually increase what you can perceive at the very edges of your vision.

Keeping your vision expanded, slowly lower your gaze to the horizontal. Notice how much more you can see. Use this technique to set your focus when entering social gatherings, and you will take in lots of information without looking stressed or intense.

Learning to Read People

When the eyes say one thing, and the tongue another,
a practiced man relies on the language of the first.
                    Ralph Waldo Emerson

The first rule in reading the language of the body is that the context means everything. Someone crossing their arms might be an indication of defensiveness; then again they might be cold or have a curry stain on their shirt. Each person has unique non-verbals and the meanings of these are dependent on their culture and upbringing. A single gesture, change in proximity, look or movement is impossible to interpret on its own or out of context. The secret is to look for clusters of signs.

As we have said, your interpretation of body language is largely unconscious. While you get a sense of what someone means, you don't give too much conscious thought to the messages. You have more of an overall feeling rather than a considered translation of each signal. Now, with some added insight, you'll be more tuned in to picking up the signals and interpreting the messages. As you understand and practice these methods, you'll become a skilled observer and people-watcher, and will develop your intuition even further.

Observing Body Language
Start being more aware of people's body language. Keep a notebook and write down any non-verbal signals, clues

or messages you observe in different situations and between different groups of people.

The more you observe the same people's body language in different situations, the greater your understanding of non-verbal signals will develop.

- Work mates—notice how their body language changes when the boss is around.
- Friends—notice their body language when you are in an established group of friends compared with when some new person they fancy enters the group.
- Family—because you know them more intimately, observe how their body language reflects their moods.
- Couples in love—what does their body language say about how they are relating?
- Couples in conflict—notice the signals their bodies are sending.

Advertisers use body language to sell their products. Just look through the pages of any magazine and work out how they are doing this. Ask yourself, "What is this signaling?"

Closing the Gap

Have you ever experienced someone who invades your personal space without being invited? You know, those people who stand too close and seem to have no idea that space is personal. We all have a different idea about what is too close and that changes depending on how we feel about the person standing nearby. What is a constant is that the more you like someone, the closer you'll let them get. So the secret in flirting is to close the gap in a way that makes them feel comfortable. This requires a good radar—the ability to pick up those non-verbals, plus a playful curiosity to see how far you can go.

Edward T. Hall, who researched perception and the use of space, believes that Americans, the English and Australians have four distinct personal space zones. The public zone starts at about 12 feet and extends to the limit of sight. The social zone reaches from 3 to 12 feet. The personal zone ranges from 2 to 4 feet. The intimate zone is from zero (touching) to 2 feet. Therefore space or proximity has meaning and if someone breaches our personal bubble we can feel uncomfortable, tense or resentful, although we may not be aware of the cause.

These zones vary dramatically with culture and circumstances. Circumstances that create variations in the zones include elevators and public transportation. Most people cope with the reduction in their personal space in these places by avoiding eye contact. If you smile and look at people in an elevator or on public transportation you'll be considered a little strange—unless of course you know how to flirt effectively, in which case it can be a lot of fun.

Our advice is that when you want to flirt with someone, take your time and start at the edge of their personal zone (about 4 feet away) and keep your body turned away from them at an angle of about 45 degrees. The advantages of the angled body position are that it is less threatening and it allows you to observe a lot with your peripheral vision.

If they move closer to you then you can take that as a signal. If they don't move closer, wait until you have engaged their interest and made them feel comfortable before you move in closer. Be careful to watch their eyes—if they narrow that indicates the person feels threatened and you will need to back off. Unlike other signals, the narrowing of the eyes is global, not cultural, and it sends a clear message on its own.

When you have built rapport with someone and you are having a great time flirting, try moving or swaying just slightly back. If things are going as well as you think they are then the other person will unconsciously close the gap.

Personal Space

Here's a fun and eye-opening exercise to try next time you are with a group of friends.

Two people should stand 16 feet apart and look each other in the eye. They then move toward each other, slowly, one step at a time.

As you do this notice how it feels as you come closer: are you comfortable? What issues come up for you when people get closer? Does it feel different with different people?

A note about laughter: Some people break into laughter during this exercise. Laughter is a way of releasing tension. If you or your partner laugh, think about what caused the tension.

Body Talks

For great flirts, like our friend Anthony, flirting is a state of mind and body. He has made the unconscious conscious, fine-tuned his skills and inserted them back into his unconscious mind so they have become part of who he is. It is his body language, his gestures, the way he moves through a room or perches on the arm of a chair. He no longer thinks about his body language because he now trusts his body will give out the right messages.

Anthony flirts with the world around him. He is in his forties—tall, skinny and not particularly handsome (in fact, his looks are those only a mother could love)—but his charm is magnetic. Watching him walk into a party is like watching a celebrity enter a crowd. He connects with everyone there by acknowledging them personally, even if it is just with a glance in their direction or a tilt of his head.

Anthony has the ability to make each person feel they are the most important person in the room. His movements are fluid and slow; he often seems to melt toward you when he speaks to you. Watching Anthony you realize his body language sends a warm, sensual message, so it is not surprising to see women fall for him or for men to seek him out as a friend. He has made the body language of flirting a natural part of how he moves through life.

Our bodies send out messages constantly and often we don't recognize that we're communicating a lot more than we think. The secret is to become aware of what your body is saying. Once you are aware you can begin to communicate non-verbally with intent.

Dr. Monica Moore, professor of behavioral and

social sciences at Webster University in Missouri, in 1985 catalogued fifty-two non-verbal communications used by women in social settings in her study Non-verbal Courtship Patterns in Women. Her research showed that the more signals a woman gives out, the more likely she is to get a response from men. She also found that the women who were using a variety of different signals rather than repeating the same signal over and over got more responses.

During the research, Dr. Moore also noticed that men waited until they had a number of signals from a woman before they responded. Men are also more likely to wait for an initial signal from a woman than to make an approach without some encouragement. This indicates that in the world of flirting, women may be the initiators through their non-verbal communications.

Of the fifty-two flirting signals identified by Dr. Moore, there are twenty-one that in our experience will make you an expert non-verbal flirt. These twenty-one non-verbal flirting signals are not specific to men or women.

Twenty-One Ways to Body Flirt

1. The Scan
The room-encompassing glance is hardly a technique as this is what invariably happens early in the proceedings. It gives the glancer a chance to take a good look around the room/party/bar and figure out if there is anyone worth flirting with. It's really a talent stocktake because if there's nobody who interests you, then you might just take the opportunity to hang out with your friends. In the scan, eye contact is not made with any specific individual. The

duration of the scan is brief, from five to ten seconds. This is when your peripheral vision comes in handy.

2. Hello Hello

Save this short darting glance for when you've spotted someone worth flirting with. This glance is directed at a particular person and consists of gazing, then turning away quickly. It is usually repeated in bouts with an average of three gazes per bout. How many bouts? Well, that depends on how long it takes the object of your desire to acknowledge you and give you the green light.

3. Lock and Load

This fixed gaze is where the rubber meets the road and the flirting starts. Once you suspect that the interest might be mutual, you make prolonged eye contact (more than three seconds) and repeat this glance several times over a period of some minutes or until they make the initial approach. How often have you heard the phrase, "They caught my eye," when someone is referring to how they met? Often the first real connection between two people is prolonged eye contact. It's the fascination of discovering what lies behind the gaze that draws people together.

4. Smiling

The smile is the most frequently used and recognized non-verbal cue. A smile is non-committal but very effective. You can smile at men and women when you make eye contact and, although it doesn't have to be a prelude to flirting, it's a great starting point. Even if you have no intention of getting to know someone *really* well, smiling acknowledges you have noticed them. Smiling at someone makes them feel special and as that's what flirting is all about . . . Smiling even affects the way you talk. Telephone sales people are sometimes trained to put a mirror on their desk so that they can see themselves smiling while making calls.

5. Eyebrow Flash

Once you've got someone's attention by making eye contact, hold their gaze for a few seconds longer than you would normally. If you feel encouraged to give them a signal they can't mistake, give them the eyebrow flash. This is an exaggerated raising of both your eyebrows for a few seconds—no longer or you'll look like Groucho Marx. Combined with eye contact and a smile, it's guaranteed to get you a response. The eyebrow flash is another global non-verbal—with the notable exception of Hong Kong, where it is considered the height of rudeness.

6. Hey, Look at Me

Guys, have you ever taken notice when a girl walks past you, ostensibly on her way somewhere? If she was holding her head high, swaying her hips, holding in her stomach and arching her back so her breasts were pushed out, she was flirting. If she made eye contact with you, you were the one she was parading for. If you let her walk by and didn't give her any sign that you were interested, you missed the opportunity to flirt with her.

Girls, did you take action when that cool guy smiled at you as he swaggered past with his shoulders squared, his stomach held in, his hands in his pockets and his crotch thrust forward? How much more blatant do you want him to be? His parade was a cluster of non-verbal cues that were screaming, "Notice me—I've noticed you and I like what I see." Parading past a flirt target is all about getting yourself noticed by putting yourself on display while having a destination, such as the bar or the bathroom, in case your parade does not attract your target. Remember, a great flirt never does anything they can't back out of gracefully.

7. Approach

Before you decide to approach someone, you might like to look for some signals that they would welcome you into their personal space. If you are not too sure that you've picked up the right signals, try a combination of the nonverbal signals and see if you get a response—a returned smile might be a good cue! Okay, so you've recognized the signals and mustered the courage to walk up to someone you want to flirt with. This is possibly the most direct nonverbal sign, but damn it, you can't just stand there within a few feet of them and not say anything. Just don't blow it with some faded, sleazy pick-up line. If you've bothered to make the effort to approach them try something simple like, "Hi, I'm [your name]" or just "Hello."

8. Come On Over

This is the reverse of approaching someone. Rather than you making the approach, you signal them to join you. This can be as obvious as an open palm swept over a vacant chair or as subtle and ambiguous as a curling of the fingers with the hand held by the side. This finger curl can be used while walking past a person. They are not sure whether the signal was meant for them and so they will begin to watch you to make sure—leaving the way open for you to smile and break the ice.

9. Solitary Dance

This one is for the girls. You want that guy in the corner to ask you to dance, right? He's looking over your way and smiling but he's been doing that for the past ten minutes and still hasn't made his way over. If you really want to dance, start moving your body in time to the music. It doesn't matter if you are sitting down or standing up, sway to the music and maintain eye contact. If he doesn't get the message try signaling him to come over. If this doesn't work you might have to take matters into your own hands and approach him, or you could find yourself dancing in your seat all night long.

10. Toss, Tilt and Laugh

Head tossing is great in combination with flirtatious laughter. Picture the scene: They say something remotely funny and you toss your head back and laugh—boy, do they think they are funnier than Jerry Seinfeld. Tilting the head to one side is a great way to gauge if there is any reciprocated interest. Watch to see if they mirror you and tilt their head in the same direction. If they tilt their head even slightly, they are responding to you in a positive way and the message is clear, they are enjoying your company and wishing to strengthen the connection.

11. Hair Flip

We all know this one—it's the perennial favorite of girls with long (or come to think of it, short) hair and Hugh Grant lookalikes with hair that flops in their eyes. Not restricted to pushing hair out of your face, this technique is either a languid seductive hand movement designed to make you want to run your own hands through their hair or it is a perky little flip that is flirty and fun. Either way, it's one of the most frequently used non-verbal flirting signals.

Some people, like our friend Tom, use the hair flip repeatedly. Tom flips his hair, on average, three times a minute (okay, so we counted them one day when we were watching him flirt). Sure his hair flops in his face and, come to think of it, he does look a bit like Hugh Grant, but even if he is not fully conscious of it, Tom uses the hair flip to flirt with great effect.

12. Look, I'm Vulnerable

Presenting your neck or the inside of your wrist to some-one you hardly know or have just met is like a cat rolling over and exposing its belly. It can signal a willingness to be vulnerable in the hands of the person you are presenting your neck or wrist to. Very few cats put themselves into this position unless they have good reason to trust those they expose themselves to. Alas, we humans are far more foolish when it comes to flirting, but what the hell, show a bit of neck or wrist and, if you really want to get them going, caress your neck with your fingers.

13. The Whisper

While technically not non-verbal, the body movements necessary for whispering can be used to evaporate personal space and get up close and personal. Not ready to lean in close and whisper in their ear? Then lower your voice and speak softly so they'll lean in closer to you to hear what you are saying.

14. Fondling Things (Caressing Objects)

Steve met a girl at a party who he couldn't take his eyes off. She used the "hello, hello" glance to get his attention and then started running her finger around the rim of her wineglass. Just as he was getting used to the effect, she started to caress the stem of her wineglass up and down with her index finger and thumb. By the time he got to talk to her, she had him in the palm of her hand! The "object caress" is just that, stroking, fondling or caressing any object. It can be in a sexually suggestive manner or not. Either way, playing with an object while making eye contact with someone is a powerful non-verbal flirting signal.

15. The Brush

This seemingly accidental brushing of body parts is not for the faint hearted. Sometimes it is accidental (yeah, sure it is), but more often than not it is done with explicit intent. It is frequently used in tight spots where there is not too much room to move because it can then appear to be accidental—although we know better. How many times have you brushed past someone while trying to get a drink at a crowded bar? If it's not someone you care to flirt with you move on quickly. If, on the other hand, it is someone who has "caught your eye," you'll linger just a bit, staying close enough so either of you can make a comment or start a conversation. The brush is often arm to arm, leg to leg or torso to arm contact. The bravest try for the breast brush or the pelvic brush. The instigator of the brush will often follow it with a coy apology (from a guy), or a giggle and blush combination (from a girl).

16. The Lean

We mentioned leaning forward and back earlier, when we spoke about closing the gap. The lean is often most noticeable when people are seated next to each other at a dinner party. People flirting will tend to lean toward each other. Leaning subtly changes the amount of interpersonal space and can be used to gauge interest. If you lean forward and you want to know if it's okay by them, lean back so they can close the gap. They will be unconsciously trying to maintain proximity.

17. The Touch
Unlike the brush, the touch is not accidental, nor is it to be taken as such. At some point you place your hand on the other person's arm or shoulder or knee or thigh or ... You use the touch to emphasize a point or as a sign of affection, but in reality you've seen the chance to touch a person you like or to hold their attention. For example, Sam has a way of touching a girl on the elbow that makes her feel she has his attention, even if their conversation is interrupted by a third person. Before Sam acknowledges the other person he places his hand around his companion's elbow. In this way he anchors her to him and their conversation while he is chatting to the third person. Coming back to their conversation, the girl has been "engaged" by the touch of the elbow, so she feels the connection has remained unbroken.

18. The Foot to Foot, Knee to Knee or Thigh to Thigh
The conversation is flowing well, there's no chance of the accidental brush and you are not feeling confident enough to try the touch. You're looking for something that could build up to the touch so you rub your foot against their foot ... umm, you got a good reaction to that, they didn't move away and returned just a bit of pressure. If you are feeling game wait a few minutes then rub your knee

against their knee or your thigh against their thigh. Now you've moved from flirting to seduction because there is nothing ambiguous about this signal.

19. Play

When you feel like getting playful you'll indulge in flirtatious behavior such as pinching, tickling, gentle tapping, sticking out your tongue, sitting in his/her lap, stealing his/her cap or keys. These acts are all designed to make him/her take notice of you. If you steal something like keys, what will be the likely response? Maybe you'll be chased with the excuse of retrieving the "stolen" goods.

20. Hugs

Hugs are a great way to part company and a fantastic way to leave an impression. The hug is not suitable for all occasions but if you get the opportunity don't blow it with either a weak or overly sexual hug. A good hugger knows the secret is to get heart to heart, hold firm without squeezing and to take a long, slow, deep breath. This will build a deep connection and pave the way for future flirting.

21. Kissing

Lips to lips, cheek to cheek or kissing the air—the dilemma here is which kiss for what occasion? This is another of those personal space issues. Our advice is that a light kiss on each cheek—very European—is almost always accepted after suitable introduction. Ladies, if you want to give him a green light or just collect another adoring male, an unexpected peck on his cheek will send him in a spin.

So now you know the twenty-one flirting signals you can use or look for. Remember, nothing means anything on its own. When clusters of non-verbal flirting signals are combined with flirtatious language it's an intoxicating cocktail.

The twenty-one flirting signals are adapted from Dr. Monica Moore's studies which can be found at www.webster.edu/ depts/artsci/bass/faculty/m_m.html.

Key Points

- You are constantly sending signals via your body language.
- Most of these signals are sent unconsciously.
- Observe non-verbal signals and look for clusters of signals that send a similar message.
- Develop your peripheral vision.
- Be aware of personal space, observe it with others and use it to gauge interest.
- Flirts take notice of the non-verbal signals.

SEVEN

Word Power

You can tell whether a man is clever by his answers.
You can tell whether a man is wise by his questions.

Naguib Mahfouz

Getting your tongue around luscious language will make you a fabulous flirt. Language can be persuasive and/or suggestive; it will change moods, yours and other people's. Does this mean you need to carry a dictionary and a thesaurus around with you? No, of course not. However, in flirting, being playful with words pays dividends.

If you have found yourself tongue-tied when flirting don't despair, we are going to give you plenty of ideas and exercises to make you fluent. After reading this chapter, cheesy pick-up lines will be a thing of the past; instead you'll be able to engage anyone, anywhere, anytime.

Words are powerful, they can wound or heal, build up, tear down, compliment or criticize. Words create pictures, sounds and feelings in the mind of the listener. They can create or enhance emotions. Language is a code for thoughts, ideas and feelings. When someone hears you speak, their mind has to actively de-code what they hear. The very act of de-coding changes the connections between brain cells, so physically and literally it "changes someone's mind."

While the exact words you used often disappear from memory, what remains is the meaning. It is the meaning that matters most. It is the meaning that creates a feeling, an impression. By using language to have fun with people, you'll make them feel good and leave an impression that you're a great person to be around.

We have been asked, "Is persuasive and suggestive language manipulative?" The answer is yes, but not in a negative way. If you have a way of making people feel appreciated, wouldn't you use it?

Opportunities to flirt fluently are everywhere once you open your mind to them. When you flirt you are seeking to engage someone, to grab and hold their attention in a positive, playful way. So how do you do that?

Sophie saw him in the canned food aisle. He was tall, lean and quite handsome, but what really attracted her was his "little boy lost" look as he puzzled over which canned tuna to put in his basket. Sophie didn't make a habit of flirting with strangers but she found herself stopping next to "canned tuna guy."

"This one's very good," she found herself saying as she took a can from the shelf. He turned to her, a little surprised but obviously pleased to have some help. "Thanks," he said. "Maybe I'll stock up," and he grabbed six cans.

"Guess you must like fish," said Sophie with a smile.

Canned tuna guy returned the smile but before he answered, he checked out the contents of Sophie's cart, in which there were four containers of detergent. "And you must like washing." He grinned.

Sophie looked up at him a little sheepishly and explained the benefits of buying that particular brand of detergent in bulk. When she had finished, there was a slight pause as they stood there looking at each other. It was canned tuna guy who broke the silence. "You've convinced me. Which aisle do I get some from?"

"You seem like a nice guy, I'll show you," said Sophie, and the two of them continued to shop together, sometimes parting ways but managing to "bump" into each other again at various times.

Sophie wasn't sure who it was that suggested coffee, but they found themselves at the coffee shop next door where they chatted for two hours. At the time of writing this Sophie and Tim (canned tuna guy) are still dating.

Flirting doesn't always lead to dating, and nor should it, but sometimes it does and it's fun to hear how two people get together. The meeting between Sophie and Tim demonstrates that each flirting moment has a form and if we analyze it we can uncover the anatomy.

Sophie flirted with a great opening line that utilized what she had observed—Tim's bachelor shopping style.

Utilization is jargon for saying what is undeniably so—
this builds rapport and a bridge to further conversation.

Next Sophie asked a question, "Guess you must like
fish?" Although phrased as a statement this contains some
humor. Tim chose not to answer the question but picked
up the flirting by noticing the contents of Sophie's cart.
After her explanation Sophie used the pause for great
effect; again Tim picked up the cue and asked where he
could get some of the detergent Sophie seemed so fond of.
Sophie's flattery, although not too over the top, was
enough for Tim to get the message. Tim and Sophie both
had fun and began to feel the energy between them—the
rest is becoming history.

Knowing the anatomy of a flirting moment enables you
to "unpack" flirting language skills and to see where you
might make some improvements to your own style. Pulling
apart the structure of a fluent flirting moment may make
it appear to lose its magic, even feel cold and mechanical,
but after you have learned the steps you'll become as fluid
as a dancer who has perfected their technique and then
lost themselves to the music.

The Anatomy of a Flirting Moment

There are six elements to a flirting moment. They are:
creating rapport, asking questions, using flattery, using
humor, pausing and creating energy.

Create Rapport

We have covered this in chapter five, but if you are making
contact for the first time creating rapport is essential. You

can use a phrase stating the obvious (known as utilization). This could be an observation of fact or behavior, something that is undeniable and therefore must be agreed upon. An example would be, "It's noisy in here, isn't it?" or, "I see you are drinking a gin and tonic." This builds common ground and a foundation for flirting. A good start when meeting new people is to use two or three statements before moving onto a question.

"I noticed you are reading..."

"Gee, it's busy in here tonight."

"Good venue for a function."

Ask Questions

Be curious. Asking questions allows you to gather information about people which you can use while flirting with them. Remember in the movie *Shrek* where the ogre explains to the donkey that ogres are like onions? People are like onions too, each question you ask reveals another layer. Ask open-ended and, preferably, unusual questions. The art of word power is about getting the other person to open up about him- or herself.

Listen and pay attention so you'll remember the personal stuff. Great flirts know the power of showing a keen interest in other people and remembering what they've been told. Asking questions not only keeps the conversation flowing, it allows you to steer it in the direction you want to go.

Don't ask questions that can be answered with either a yes or a no, such as, "Do you come here often?" Also avoid clichés "like the plague"! Instead you could ask, "What is it you like about this place?" The answer can't be a yes or a no and will tell you something more about the other person and allow you to keep the conversation flowing.

Keep your questions open and "soft," meaning easy to answer, for instance, "Do you mind if I ask you a question?" This type of question is never refused because you have already asked them a question about answering a question and most people are conditioned to be polite and helpful. To create flow in the conversation use your keen powers of observation to ask a question that extends from the statements you used to create rapport.

Something to be aware of is that if someone asks you a question, you don't have to answer it immediately. You can answer a question with a question. This lets you direct the conversation and keep it flirty. If you are going to answer their question with a question of your own, link it with a softening statement, such as, "Great question, but before I answer can I ask you..." or, "Wow, nobody's ever asked me that before. What made you ask me?"

Good questions are at the heart of flirting.

Have a go at creating your own flirting questions by completing the following:

> Maybe I could ask you first...
> How do I ask you...
> How do I tell you...
> How would I know...
> What would it take...
> What can I do...
> What's different about...

In chapter five we talked about verbally matching to get
in step. We have included below a list of question starters
from which you can create powerful flirting moments. For
example, "How do I tell you that you look fantastic
without you thinking I'm coming on to you?" These very
useful questions get to the heart of the matter and uncover
interests, beliefs and values.

- What does that mean to you?
- What do you believe about . . . ?
- What do you think about . . . ?
- How important is that to you?
- What is the most fascinating/exciting thing about . . . ?
- What do you want to do about . . . ?
- How do you want to see this turn out?

When the person answers, pay full attention to their
answer and ask them another question that follows on
from their answer.

If they stall you can ask another question. When people
are asked these sorts of questions it gets them in touch with
how they feel, so a word of warning: when flirting don't
use these questions around a painful topic. Asking someone to talk about a painful relationship break-up and
getting them to re-experience all the anguish will not
endear you to them. Remember that you want the take-
away experience of talking to you to be one of pleasure
not pain. Use these questions to get people in touch with
good experiences and they will remember you as someone
who makes them feel good.

If you don't want to get too deep and meaningful, keep
the subjects general initially. What kind of movies do
you like? What music do you listen to? What books or

magazines do you like to read? You'll be amazed what you can learn about a person from these things, especially if you probe just a little.

"You like romance novels. So tell me, why do you enjoy them?"

"What is it about Eminem's lyrics that you like?"

"Horror movies, really? Mmmm, so what attracts you to horror movies?"

Twenty Questions

As a kid you might have played a game called truth or dare. Someone asks you a question and you answer it truthfully or complete a dare that usually either embarrasses or frightens you. A similar game called twenty questions (usually played without the dare consequence) is even more fun to play as an adult, especially when flirting.

You agree to ask each other any number of questions (usually up to twenty), which will be answered truthfully. To make it more interesting you can agree that once a question is asked the other person cannot ask it. Nitty Gritty is a board game (www.nittygrittygame.com) that expands on the twenty questions model. It's a great way to practice asking questions and flirting. There are some terrific questions, so good in fact that we have included some in our list.

- Do you cry at sad movies?
- Who is the person you most wanted to have a fling with but didn't?

- What is your worst habit?
- If you could spend a week in someone else's body whose would it be?
- What do you think is the least forgivable thing your partner could do?
- Do you believe monogamy works?
- If you found $50,000 buried in a box in the wilderness would you keep it?
- What part of your body is the most ticklish?
- How many pillows do you like to sleep with?
- Have you ever sunbathed naked in public?
- What is your favorite thing to reduce stress?
- What is your favorite thing to do on a Sunday?
- Has anyone ever taken a photo of you naked?
- What is your favorite part of the body to touch?
- Are you competitive?
- Do you snore?
- What is the silliest thing you own?
- Have you ever lied about your profession to pick up someone?
- If you could have plastic surgery for free on any part of your body, what would you have done?
- Do you consider yourself a flirt?
- Would you pose naked for an art class?
- What comic strip makes you laugh the most?
- A genie grants you one wish—what would it be?
- Who do you admire most in the world (living or dead)?
- In your opinion what is the one thing the opposite gender needs to learn?

- If you wanted to turn on your lover as quickly as possible what would you do?
- What part of your body do you love to have massaged?
- What is your favorite thing to do to have fun?
- If you could get on a plane today, where would you go?
- Where is the one place you haven't visited but would love to see?
- What is your favorite comedy movie?
- Do you have a tattoo, birthmark or secret piercing?

In the following story notice how Kim uses questions to connect with Greg and take their flirting to the next level.

Kim had just met Greg and they were getting on famously, then Kim decided it was time to get to the heart of the matter to see what made Greg tick.

"Tell me about you," she asked with a cheeky grin.

"Not much to tell," he said modestly.

"Sure there is, tell me what you like to do for fun."

Greg smirked.

"Other than *that*, how do you relax?"

"Well, I like to go to the movies."

"The movies. Great, me too. What do you like about going?"

"It's an escape, I mean, I get to step out of this world and into another."

"Mmmm," encouraged Kim.

"In fact, what I really enjoy is sneaking off to the movies in the afternoon, it makes me feel like a schoolboy playing hooky."

"Really?"

"Yep. And I really like it when you go in and it's daylight and you come out and it's dark—it's like I've been in some kind of time warp."

"Cool," said Kim as she lightly touched his arm. "And what else?"

"That's it really," said Greg, who seemed to be in a bit of a daze as if he had just come out of a cinema.

"So do you like to go by yourself or with someone?"

"I like to do both, but it has to be someone special. I mean going to the movies, well, it's like a date isn't it?"

"Is it?" Kim raised her eyebrows.

"Say would you like to do a movie with me?" Greg asked excitedly.

"What, you mean play hooky and feel kinda naughty?"

"If you like . . ."

As Kim and Greg go off to the movies, are you ready to ask some flirty questions yourself? Remember, when someone goes "inside" themselves to search for the answer they'll re-experience some of the feelings associated with the question. A good flirt knows how to link good feelings to themselves and Kim did this beautifully with a light touch on Greg's arm. The eyebrow raise was a clear nonverbal green signal that even slow-moving Greg couldn't miss. It's all pretty easy really, when you pay attention.

Did you pick up on some of Greg's interests and values? Greg was initially modest or reserved in sharing about himself, but the obvious double meaning of "what [do] you like to do for fun?" set a frame for something to talk about. Kim's question then changed to "how do you relax?"

Greg tells Kim that he values the movies because they give him a chance to "escape" and make him feel like a schoolboy. What we can guess from this is that Greg has strong values about behaving properly and that to have fun or relax he needs to escape the confines of work. Greg mentions the time warp effect of the cinema, so he probably has a strong value based on being on time.

By stepping into Greg's shoes, Kim started to "get" him and build a connection that made Greg feel comfortable enough to ask for a date. While a date is not always the intention of flirting, in this case it made them both feel good.

Flatter Flirtatiously

It would be reasonable to expect those most prone to flattery would be people with low self-esteem. Not so. The higher your self-esteem, the more likely you are to regard flattery and compliments as fair and just praise for your talents and beauty. The challenge you face when using flattery and compliments when flirting is to make them genuine and sincere.

We use so many superlatives in our everyday language that they have become worn out from over use. Following a compliment with an infrequently asked question will open up a conversation and enable you to build deep rapport and appear genuine. For example, "I've watched you solve difficult situations between work colleagues. You have the most amazing talent for leaving everyone feeling good about themselves. Can you teach me how to handle such problems and get the same positive outcomes you do?"

Tried and Tested Flattery Tips

Casanova believed the way to successful flirtation was to praise the beautiful for their intelligence and the intelligent for their beauty.

Flatter someone to another person and it is likely the compliment will be passed on. This is a very effective way to get the attention of the person you flattered and it is almost certain the compliment will be taken as genuine and sincere *because* you were speaking to a third person. Don't spoil this, though, by asking the person to pass on the compliment!

If you use general or one-size-fits-all compliments such as "You're great," or "You're the best," you could be flattering anyone. Be specific. Instead of telling someone you think they are great, tell them *why* you think they are great. For example, "I really like the way you take time to listen to others' opinions before sharing your thoughts," or "The way you play with your hair makes you look so cute."

Your ability to compliment and flatter is in direct relation to your ability to observe. That's what flirting is all about—noticing other people and making them feel good. So forget the backhanded personal compliment, such as "I'm surprised at how nice you are. Everybody told me you were a real pain." Backhanders are a mixed message and the recipient is more likely to pick up on the negative and discount the positive. It also suggests your original opinion of them was less than complimentary.

You may get away with using a bit of negativity when you are complimenting a situation rather than a person. Say someone you like invites you to an art-house film but you prefer Hollywood blockbusters. If you enjoy the film you might tell them you always thought art-house films were weird and obscure but thanks to them you've now found out you like them.

Nobody gets tired of being complimented but the warm and fuzzy feeling you get when someone pays you a compliment only lasts so long. It doesn't matter whether you repeat the compliment if it is personal, sincere and fits well.

Sharing a secret with someone is a subtle form of flattery. You are letting them know you trust them with something intimate about yourself. Be careful you choose someone you know well enough to trust with your secret, otherwise this could backfire big time.

Use Ambiguity or Humor

Nothing succeeds like humor; it is one of the most prized qualities looked for in a relationship. If you have ever read the singles' columns you'll see GSOH—good sense of humor (although we have it on good authority that it can also stand for good salary/own home)—is regularly listed as a desired attribute or requirement. A GSOH is not necessarily just about telling jokes; it is more about a sense of playfulness and seeing the funny side of daily situations and the funny things people say and do. Being able to laugh at yourself is very attractive as long as it is not a put-down. In flirting keep it light—if you lose your sense of humor your attempts to flirt will fall flat.

Tim was standing at the crossing waiting for the traffic lights to go red and the little man to turn green. Taped to the light post was a flyer for a psychic with tear-off telephone numbers at the bottom. Tim turned to the girl next to him, smiled, and pointed to the poster. "If the psychic was any good she would already know my number," he quipped. Perhaps this is not the funniest or most original line you have ever heard but at least Tim had a go and the girl smiled and everybody felt a bit better for the joke.

Flirtatious Double Entendres

A double entendre, or double meaning, adds playfulness and lots of ambiguity to your flirting. It is a word or phrase open to two interpretations—one clean and the other usually *risqué* or indelicate. Double entendres are naughty but also clever. Delivered in the true spirit of flirting they add humor and wit to your conversations.

Elliott White Springs, in 1947, shocked the U.S. business community with his double entendre using his company's name Springmaid. Making use of a double meaning to sell his sheets, he used a cartoon of a Native North American couple on a sheet hammock. The caption read, "A buck well spent on a Springmaid sheet."

The fun of using double meanings in your flirting lies in the ambiguity, not in the obvious. Being good with the double entendre is about the delivery as it is easy to get carried away and become crude rather than funny.

The following article by Jill Phythian was posted on the BBC1 Web site, h2g2:

Key components of a successful double entendre include use of indeterminate pronouns such as "it" and "one," plenty of prepositions such as "up" and "in," and handy little verbs like "have" and "get." A keen double entendre user will never raise a flag when he could simply get it up, or complicate a situation when he could just make it hard. It is important to remember that your expression should have some ostensibly clean interpretation, however unlikely—if this is omitted, you end up with a single entendre, which lacks style. Certain conversational topics are guaranteed double entendre zones: These include cookery (sausages, bananas etc.), architecture (gussets, cleats and erections) and engineering (knobs, gearsticks and lots of parts that get very stiff if you don't grease them properly).

It is traditional to show that you recognize a double entendre by calling out one of a number of possible response lines. Popular responses include "oo-er," "nudge, nudge, wink, wink!" or simply "sounds a bit rude!" It is also possible to add those sentences as suffixes yourself, although purists disdain such crass usage, preferring to just slip one in wherever possible.

Double entendres are indispensable when flirting or presenting gameshows, and not recommended at funerals or international summit meetings.

Timing and Delivery

Never underestimate the use of a pause to create space in a conversation. The pause allows the other person to finish a sentence or to contribute. This is a great way to get you both on the same page—so to speak—and when this happens the flirting will flow naturally between you.

Create the Energy

Have you watched a great rally at Wimbledon? The more times the ball goes over the net, the greater the energy, the greater the excitement and anticipation. Flirting fluently is about keeping the ball in play by using words.

The more banter the greater the flirting.

Communication is a skill you can learn. It's like riding a bicycle or typing.

If you're willing to work at it, you can rapidly improve the quality of every part of your life.

Brian Tracy

Key Points

- Great flirts love words.
- Use words to be playful and to keep the banter going.
- Learn how to ask the right questions.
- Pay compliments and flatter.
- Notice the little things and remember personal stuff.

EIGHT

Recognizing Personal Filters

You can't figure someone out if you don't know the world they live in.

Dr. Michael Hall

Your personal interpretations and perceptions are powerful filters you put on everyday situations. It is not just extraordinary life experiences that change the way we interpret and perceive things, it is also the repetition of everyday events and outcomes that set our personal patterns. The same is true in flirting. Your body language, what you say and how you behave will always be received, translated and processed through the other person's personal filters.

Say Brad thinks of something and decides to communicate it to Julie. Consciously, Brad translates the thought into words to describe it. Meanwhile Brad's unconscious mind is transmitting how the thought makes him feel by causing him to send non-verbal signals as well. Brad speaks the words and Julie hears them; Julie translates the words into thoughts via pictures, sounds and feelings. The translation Julie makes is affected by how she filters information, how she is feeling at the time and her past experiences.

Julie is also unconsciously picking up Brad's non-verbal signals and trying to interpret them. Her interpretation may or may not be accurate but it will definitely affect how she translates the words, therefore what she thinks they mean.

Even if Brad is absolutely clear about what he wants to communicate, is it any wonder Julie might get the wrong idea? This situation is further complicated by the fact that Brad may not be entirely clear about how he feels and what he wants to get across.

It sounds complicated but we have been communicating like this since we learned to talk. Understanding this model will help you to decipher messages and to have a choice in sending clear messages, or not, as the flirting situation dictates.

The Two Channels

When you watch television you are informed or enter-
tained by the pictures and the soundtrack. Have you ever
watched a movie with the sound turned off and tried to
guess what's going on? Or had the TV on in one room
while you were in another, listening to the program but
not able to see the pictures?

To really understand what's going on we need both
pictures and sound. It's the same when we communicate.
There are two channels: verbal (or spoken) and non-verbal
(or body language). You use these two channels to transmit
your thoughts and feelings.

To transmit thoughts you tend to use the verbal channel
because thoughts are most easily expressed through words.
When you want to transmit feelings you may still use the
verbal channel to express your thoughts about how you feel
but the most powerful messages come through your body
language or non-verbal signals. Think of your thoughts as
your head and your feelings as your heart. (We will expand
further this concept of head and heart in the next chapter.)

Your brain is overloaded by information during every
waking moment. It copes by filtering out most of the
information and only paying attention to the things it
perceives as being important. Filters are mostly unconscious. An example of this would be a crowded party
where everybody is talking in groups; you are able to hear
the people in your immediate circle but the other groups
are filtered out and they become just a babble of sound.
However, when someone in one of the other groups starts
to talk about you and uses your name, your attention
swings to them and you hear what they are saying because

the filter is removed and your attention is shifted. An example of visual filters is what happens when you buy a car. The moment you start shopping for, or driving, that type of car, you notice every second car on the road seems to be that same model and brand.

The exercise in chapter five helped you work out if you are predominantly a looker, listener or feeler. These preferences act like a filter. The content of a message will be filtered depending on the receiver's primary interests and values. Understanding this gives you a key to deepen rapport with others. Feelers may filter out much of what is said and put more weight on how the speaker made them feel. Listeners will take note of what is said and how it is said and may be critical of thoughts that are not expressed well. Lookers focus on appearance and facial expressions.

Your primary interest is you. There is no need for false modesty here as it is the same for all of us. If someone is talking about you, you'll listen intently, but if they talk about their primary interest (themselves) with no reference to you, it is likely you'll switch off at some point. So when flirting *don't* talk about yourself, talk about the person you are flirting with. When you do this they'll pay attention and are less likely to misunderstand what you are trying to communicate.

After yourself, you have other primary interests that can be divided up into people, places, things, action and information. Different people place different value on these interests. A couple returning from a holiday in Greece will respond differently when asked how it went—she might talk about the great people they met around the pool and he might talk about the architecture and history of the place.

Since knowledge is power, this might be a good time to find out what your primary interest is.

Your Priorities

Circle *all* the statements that apply to you.

1. When I relax, I like to

    a. do things with friends or family
    b. learn about new people, places or things
    c. visit interesting places or just do things around home
    d. participate in sports or some other activity
    e. spend time in stores looking for something new

2. I most enjoy reading or watching

    a. biographies, gossip magazines, reality TV, entertainment, news
    b. travel guides or programs, *National Geographic*
    c. sporting magazines, extreme sports, fitness advice, do-it-yourself projects
    d. self-help books, the Discovery Channel, business news, professional publications
    e. *Vogue*, mail-order catalogs, home shows, car magazines

3. If I travel I like

    a. meeting new people
    b. taking off to explore the local area
    c. experiencing the local cultural activities and customs

d. learning about the local history and visiting places that will increase my knowledge of the area

e. buying a memento of my visit

4. I prefer to spend my leisure time

a. with friends, family or meeting new people

b. visiting different locations and exploring new places

c. playing sport or doing something active

d. going to workshops, taking courses to learn something new or reading to improve my mind

e. practicing retail therapy

5. I choose to live where I do because

a. I am close to my friends and family

b. location, location, location

c. it is close to the activities I enjoy

d. it's a good environment for learning

e. it's close to the shops

6. During the holiday season I am most likely to be found

a. hanging out with people I care about

b. at a resort, my own home, somewhere special

c. getting into something active and fun

d. taking time out to catch up on reading

e. shopping for gifts, making the house look festive

7. By choice I will eat

a. with family, friends, where I can watch people

b. at home or in my favorite restaurant

c. on the run

d. while reading or watching TV

e. at a good restaurant

8. My dream job would

   a. involve meeting and working with interesting people
   b. be in a great environment
   c. involve lots of activities
   d. provide opportunities to learn and grow personally
   e. pay well so I could spend

Count up the number of a, b, c, d and e statements that you circled. Write them below and then make a bar graph of your choices like in the example below.

Totals: a (people) _____ b (places) _____ c (activities) _____
d (knowledge) _____ e (things) _____

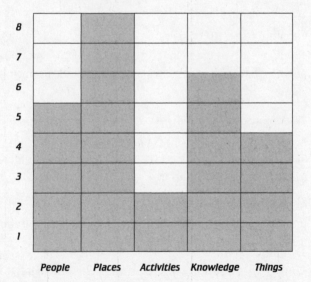

This quiz is adaped from the work of Roger Bailey. You will see your primary filters are those subjects relating to the letters you received high scores for.

Be careful not to monopolize a conversation by talking too much about what interests you. Take note of what others are talking about and focus on those subjects instead.

Primary Filters of Others

When you are talking to people you won't have the luxury of asking them to complete the above questionnaire to find out what their priorities are, so here is a guide to help you spot the primary interest of someone you are talking to.

People people (PP) care most about the who. They talk about people, their friends, people they know, famous people. They have a tendency to gossip and dislike being alone.

Places people (PLP) talk about where they have traveled and their homes (which would have to be in the "right" place). They take pride in their space, so their homes, gardens or offices would be neat or well appointed.

Action people (AP) hate just sitting around. They like feeling the rush of activity and will talk about their hobbies, sports and recreation time.

Knowledge people (KP) value the why and what of information and will talk about books they read, things they studied, courses they have taken.

Things people (TP) care about money, status and power. They talk about their possessions, cars, houses, clothes and toys.

Same/Different Filters

A very powerful filter that causes confusion in communication is evaluating new information in terms of sameness or difference. Some people process new information by looking for the exceptions or how it is not true. When you speak to these people their common reply will be, "Yes, but . . ." These people are attracted by things that are different; they are filtering for the exception.

The majority of people treat new information or situations by looking for how familiar or similar they are to what they already know. This is why food franchises are so popular; the majority of people are more comfortable with what they know than with trying new things.

What do you see when you look at the arrows in the following diagram?

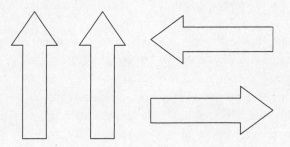

If you see four arrows that are all the same, then you filter information by looking for similarities. You look for what fits with what you already know. When you flirt, you'll be drawn to the same person or same type of person to flirt with because you feel comfortable.

If you saw two arrows in the same direction and two in different directions then you filter information by looking for similarities and then for what's different. When you flirt you'll initially be drawn to similar people, but it's the differences that excite you.

If you first saw two arrows facing in different directions then you are fully wired for differences. You live life seeking new experience to thrill you. You need the stimulation of something different and you'll take this attitude and preference when flirting.

How to Spot the Same/Different Filter in Others

Same same people often stay in one job for a while and go to the same places every weekend with the same friends. Not very adventurous.

Same but different people have tried a couple of new things and will cautiously explore new possibilities.

It's gotta be different people get bored easily and need new people, places and challenges to stimulate them. They are unlikely to stay in one job for long.

Can you see how if two people are trying to communicate and one is looking for differences and one is trying to find the similarities, things can get complicated and there can be misunderstandings?

There are many other filters that operate in everyday exchanges between people. When flirting or communicating in general, you need to be aware that the message is not the message until it has been received and understood. Next time you are talking to someone pay attention not only to what they are saying but also to how they are saying it. Be curious, especially if they seem to want to talk about a particular topic or seem to attach emotion to a subject.

In the last chapter we suggested some good questions to ask. Particularly useful questions to practice when you think something is being filtered are:

- What do you mean by that?
- Is that important to you?
- Help me understand, what exactly does that mean to you?

By asking these questions you will discover the world they live in and you will build a bridge of rapport.

> *The secret to understanding people is not mind-reading or even so-called intuition. The secret to reading someone is to show up in the moment and to listen so attentively that you recognize his or her frame of mind.*
>
> Dr. Michael Hall

Creating confusion can be a card played by a flirter. We have already mentioned double entendre but there are other ways you can send mixed messages, which we explore in the next chapter.

Key Points

- You interpret the world through your own personal filters.
- You are communicating on at least two channels—verbal and non-verbal.
- Verbal communication is filtered and affected by accompanying non-verbals.
- Your favorite subject is yourself so don't monopolize a conversation.
- Don't accept anything means anything unless you check it and then check it again.

NINE

Mixed Messages

Nothing is so simple that it cannot be misunderstood.

Freeman Teague Jr.

"I'm not sure if what you said is what I heard you say and if what I heard you say is what you mean, but if you mean what I thought I heard you say then I have no idea what to say!"

Confused? Translating flirting messages is often difficult but if you have the right attitude it can be fun. So far we've talked about flirting attitudes, body language, words, personal filters and interpretations. Now we are going to add thoughts and feelings to explore what happens when you send and receive flirting messages.

Body language is the primary way we express our feelings (heart) and words transmit concepts and ideas (head). If the head and heart are not in sync the result is an unintentional mixed message. In flirting there are intentional and unintentional mixed messages.

An Intention or Not?

An intentional mixed message is when you say something that can be backed away from comfortably without anyone's ego being dented or any nasty scenes taking place. For example, Ben, a fashion photographer, goes to all the new season's fashion shows to take photos for a well-known fashion magazine. One night he spots a new face, Lara, the designer of the collection being shown. Ben walks over to Lara and tells her how wonderful she looks in her new season's fashions. If Lara gets upset and tells Ben to stop trying to come on to her, Ben can feign surprise and say he was complimenting her in his professional capacity. On the other hand, if she wants to she can take the compliment personally; if she is interested she can flirt back. Lara can also step out of the situation, saving face if she does not get the response she was looking for.

The intentional mixed message is a flirting tool used almost as a matter of course when your start to flirt with someone new. Simply put, if you don't want to end up looking like a fool, you send out some mixed messages to get a reaction.

Unintentional mixed messages are usually a conflict

between the head (thoughts) and the heart (feelings). Often someone won't feel comfortable saying how or what they feel and their physiology will show it. They are unlikely to say, "This is making me feel uncomfortable," but their body language will scream, *"Stay away from me."* Someone may even non-verbally flirt with you while their language is cool and non-committal.

Sometimes your head and your heart don't agree, or your thoughts have not checked in with your feelings, but are still busily broadcasting to the world. Consider the woman we mentioned in chapter one who feels cheeky when she flirts, and admired and liked when someone flirts with her, but thinks women who flirt are usually shallow and men who flirt are often sleazy. This is a conflict between her head and her heart.

Other examples of unintentional mixed messages are when the person you are flirting with may find you attractive and fun but have an attitude that indicates it's not safe to flirt, or it's not appropriate, or "What if someone else sees?" They may enjoy the attention but have the belief that "these things" take time and feel you are progressing way too fast. Or they may want to get to know you but memories of hurt and rejection from the past prevent them from giving you any positive signals or encouragement.

Have you ever heard somebody say something like, "A part of me wants to, but another part of me doesn't?" This is evidence of a conflict between their head and their heart. While their mind tells them something may not be a great idea or someone may not be right for them, they are emotionally drawn to the idea or to the person.

Although people often operate predominantly from either the head or the heart, there are many times when the two come into conflict. Even if you usually process information, respond to other people and make your decisions from your head, there will be many times when your heart will be fighting to be heard above the dominance of your head. The reverse can be true if you usually operate from the heart. You will come up against times when you might really want to do something or want to be with someone but your head will be coming up with all sorts of thoughts that make you question your feelings. If this sounds like a recipe for confusion it is, for both you and anyone who is involved in the situation. These inner conflicts can be transmitted through what you say or via your body language and they cause indecision, confusion and even frustration.

One of the most common examples of this head–heart conflict is the person who always falls in love with the "bad boy" or "bad girl." Their head tells them it will end in tears but their heart aches for the adventure or the challenge or the excitement; sometimes their head will even throw out the possibility that this time it might be different.

Effective communication is 20 percent what you know and 80 percent how you feel about what you know.

Jim Rohn

You receive messages by your interpretation of the two channels we talked about, the verbal and non-verbal. If interpretation is your personal version of something, then it follows that all messages are open to misinterpretation. The following story of Paul and Sally illustrates unintentional mixed messages and how easy it is to misread a situation unless you keep checking whether or not you are getting it!

Paul is a friendly, likable guy in his thirties. He is single and lives in a small apartment complex where most of the residents know each other. Paul is pretty handy with his toolbox, always willing to help out if someone in the building has a blocked drain or a broken dishwasher. He has drilled holes in walls and hung pictures for at least half of the people who share his apartment complex.

Sally moves into an apartment beneath Paul's. She is also single and is in her late twenties. She and Paul strike up a friendship and often run into each other on the stairs or in the parking lot. They start to knock on each other's doors to borrow milk or sugar or coffee; these visits can turn into hours of easy conversation. The friendship develops into flirting and teasing.

Soon they meet for a cup of coffee and conversation, and Paul starts to help Sally fix things in her apartment. Then they started to exchange notes to arrange to meet for a pizza and a video at each other's apartments. Her notes are friendly rather than flirty, but she does add little hearts or flowers or smiley faces to the notes.

Paul figures the flirting along with the hearts, flowers and faces on the notes means Sally is interested in more than just sharing a cup of coffee or a pizza, so he suggests a sunset picnic.

Sally immediately withdraws and the friendship becomes strained. Paul is confused and after a few weeks of Sally trying to avoid him he confronts her. She tells him she is uncomfortable with the suggestion of a sunset picnic and she feels Paul is trying to come on to her. When Paul mentions the little notes covered in hearts and flowers she laughs and tells him they mean nothing romantic, they are just doodles. She tells Paul she considers him a friend and their relationship strictly platonic. She is surprised he hadn't understood that.

Paul's interpretation of Sally's friendliness, her flirting and the notes gave him all the signals he needed to convince himself that Sally was more than just a friend. In Paul's world, was it the hearts on the notes or the notes themselves, the flirting or the shared pizza and video nights that spurred him on to suggest a romantic date? In Sally's world, doodles of hearts and flowers were the stuff of schoolgirl notes between friends, pizza with a pal was better than a night on your own and flirting ... well didn't everyone flirt? Was Sally flirting? We think so. She was making Paul feel special and getting a buzz in return. Why then did Paul think she wanted more? And how could Sally have avoided an embarrassing situation?

Situations like this arise because one or both parties don't understand the game. Flirting is fun and reaps rewards. Where Sally was a little naive was in not realizing that unless boundaries have been set, most men see any positive message as a green light to progress further. Guys can behave like over-energetic puppies; when a girl indicates "come here" they'll jump up on her shoulders, knocking her over.

Flirting can have a tendency to escalate. Sally should have been aware of changes in Paul's enthusiastic body language and behavior. If Sally was really sure she didn't want the friendship to progress she could have given clear signals by making comments such as, "We're just having fun aren't we?" or "It's great to have a male friend to flirt with and know it won't go further than flirting." The question is whether Sally was really clear about it being just a friendship. There could have been some conflict between her head and her heart. If her heart was saying, "This is just friendship," and her head was saying, "Paul has a lot of what I'm looking for in a partner," she might have been sending more green lights than she realized to poor unsuspecting Paul.

So where did Paul go wrong? Well, Paul is not alone; lots of people make the mistake of "all or nothing." Many people have a hard time coming to grips with the flirting dance (two steps forward one step back) or they look for an outcome rather than enjoying flirting for flirting's sake.

So Paul misread the signals, perhaps because he was only paying attention to one of the two channels. When words are saying one thing and the body is saying something else, this is the time to get clarification.

Karl Grammar, a world-famous specialist on behavior, has conducted research confirming what men have long suspected—women give men a combination of signals. His findings suggest there are two reasons for this; women take time to assess a man's suitability and they want to avoid outright rejection of unsuitable men to save the men's feelings.

A woman who is sending out mixed signals is often playing for time. Even if she is not physically attracted to the man or feels there is no chemistry, she will take the time to go through a series of unconscious processes to establish his suitability. While she does this, she will send out positive signals (60 percent of the time) balanced with negative signals (about 40 percent) until she has made a firm decision as to the level of interest she has in the man. This might sound unfair, but women process information differently than men when it comes to selecting a potential mate, be it for life or for the night. She will respond to what she sees, hears and feels, and this can take some time. Men's selection process takes a considerably shorter time because their initial decision is based only on what they see.

So the challenge for guys is to understand that the signals girls send early in an encounter are always mixed. It's a lot like the pushmi-pullyu creature in *Doctor Dolittle*. With girls it is a case of "Come here ... no, not so close ... go away just a bit ... come here ... that's far enough for now, but don't go too far away ... come back." This sequence of come here and go away is totally confusing to the guys unless they understand the game.

When a woman is interested in a man she will give him a few signals, but it is not until she senses his interest in her that she really starts the process of assessing how interested in him she is and what her level of interest might be. This complicated process can take some time and some convoluted mental and emotional gymnastics. She will play possible scenarios over in her mind while she decides if this guy is the buddy kind of friend or the boyfriend kind of friend. While making this decision she is likely to give enough positive signals for him to feel confident that she is returning his interest.

Getting Clarity

So how do you handle this minefield? Just being aware that you might be getting mixed signals will improve your flirting skills. Be prepared to look for that cluster of signals we mentioned earlier and try a few initial flirtatious gestures or comments to gauge the response. If you get a good response keep looking for enough positive signals to start some serious flirting.

Start to vary the pace, two steps forward one step back—remember the rhythm of flirting. The rhythm will help you keep the flirting light-hearted and playful.

It's important to enjoy flirting for flirting's sake; like life, flirting is a journey of discovery, not a destination you have to reach. If you find people are regularly misinterpreting you then you may be guilty of sending mixed messages. You might need to sit down and have a "meeting" between your head and your heart. Is a part of you wanting more out of relationships and a part of you afraid? Just being aware this conversation is taking place between your head and your heart goes a long way to fixing the confusion. If the problem persists, talk to a coach or a friend who can help you clarify what it is you really want.

Take a look at our list of green light and red light signals and add any of your own; this will help you identify when it's okay to move forward in the game of flirting.

Some Green Light Signals
Non-verbal
- glance in your direction
- eye contact and smiling
- winking (yes, seriously—it's a really flirty thing to do especially if it is discreet)
- laughing

- holding your gaze
- playing with hair while looking at you
- rearranging clothing
- tilting the head
- fondling an object such as a glass or a set of keys
- licking or wetting the lips
- parading past you
- positioning themselves so they catch your eye often
- asking for help
- whispering
- talking to your best pal while casting glances at you
- moving in time to the music
- turning body toward you
- pointing their foot toward you if they are sitting
- touching you on the arm, leg, shoulder, elbow or back

Verbal
- I'm up for that
- ready and willing
- why don't you find out
- guess
- how could I say no?
- it must be fate
- let's find out

Some Red Light Signals
Non-verbal
- crossed arms
- yawning
- looking bored

- eyes flitting around the room or over your shoulder
- tapping fingers on a hard surface
- turning away from you
- moving away if you move closer
- shrinking from your touch

Verbal

- I'm not ready
- not right now
- I don't think so
- I can't agree
- you must be joking
- not in this lifetime

Example of Signals in Action

He looks
She makes eye contact and acknowledges
He meets eye contact and acknowledges
She smiles
He smiles
She touches her hair or does the hair flip
He approaches
Verbal flirting begins

Key Points

- Look for clusters of signals that reinforce the message you think is being sent.

- Great flirts connect with their head and their heart.
- Take everything in context.
- Make it clear to others when it is just flirting and nothing more.
- Know and work with your priorities.

TEN

Outta Sight

> *What will he say today, I wonder. I turn on my computer, I wait impatiently as it boots up, I go on-line, and my breath catches in my chest until I hear three little words: You've got mail.*
>
> Meg Ryan in *You've Got Mail*

Out of sight flirting is bold and direct. When you are not face to face you feel braver. The telephone, e-mail and chat rooms are great places to flirt and now, in what looks to be the biggest surge in flirting, there is cell phone text messaging. Is it because the consequences of an over-the-top text message are not considered to be as embarrassing as saying something stupid when you are standing in front of someone, or is it because of the convenience and immediacy? We think it is all these things. In e-mail and text message flirting you also have time on your side. You can take an hour to compose a brilliantly witty text message or e-mail.

Text Messages

Text message flirting is an icebreaker; it makes flirting fun, even for the painfully shy. Texting means there is no pressure on the sender or the receiver. It's hi-tech flirting and it is often referred to as textual intercourse. It's a no-stress way to flirt, especially if you get tongue-tied when you first meet someone.

People will text message things that they would not feel comfortable saying face to face. Text messages are not as intrusive as a phone call as they don't require the recipient to answer a call and have a conversation. It is a great way to let someone know you are thinking of him or her in the middle of a busy day. It can take away some of the awkwardness of what to say, and the limit of 160 characters in a message means clever abbreviations or emoticons are used.

Some Text Message Statistics
There is no disputing its popularity. Text message use has grown throughout the world at a rate that continues to grow

exponentially. In some markets text message use jumped by over 1000 percent from the years 2000 to 2003, when it became possible to send text messages across carriers.

While an estimated 300 million text messages are sent in Australia each month, over 25 million text messages are sent daily by just 400, 000 people in India. In the UK one million text messages are sent every hour. The USA has, until recently, lagged behind other countries in the use of text messaging, mainly because of our hybrid implementation of mobile phone technology. Their non-use of GSM (Global System for Mobile telecommunications) is also a contributing factor.

Not all text messages are used for flirting, but there is evidence to suggest that flirting messages account for a relatively high percentage of all text messages. On Valentine's Day 2002, over 80 million text messages were sent in the UK and a similarly staggering number were sent in all countries where text message services are available.

Research showed that:

- more than 50 percent of their users flirt via text message
- more than 53 percent of their single users have used text messaging to ask someone out
- one in four thinks they can be more forward in a text message than when they are talking with someone
- one in three guys said they would make their first move through a text message
- one in five girls said they would make their first move through a text message

Marketing slogans, such as "had any good text lately," or "had any cheap text lately," are in line with what the results of the research suggest. In a recent survey in Britain over 40 percent of people asked said they had used text messaging to tell someone they fancied them or to invite them out.

"Text me" is the new catchphrase. RUIT (are you in touch) with text messaging? It's the L8est way to KIT (keep in touch) and if you don't know how to text message YBS (you'll be sorry). Text messaging is a whole new language and one that's worth learning if you are at all serious about flirting. Just in case you are a text message novice, we have listed a few of the better known abbreviations in our text message dictionary below.

How far can flirting with text messages go and why have we included text message flirting in this book? Our research has shown it to be one of the most commonly used flirting tools right now. You just need to take a look at the opportunities that exist to flirt via text message to know its popularity and earning power. Text message flirting is big business. There are a plethora of companies offering an extensive variety of text message services such as Verizon, AT&T, T-Mobile, Sprint and Cingular.

Twenty-two-year-old Amber tells us that in her social circle you either receive and send text messages or you are left out of the loop. Everything from making arrangements to meet, being asked out on a date and canceling dates is done via text message. "There is more freedom to flirt via text message," she says. "I will text things I'd be too shy to ever say face to face." Amber and her current boyfriend arranged their first date via text message after meeting at a friend's party. Amber explained, "Dave was pretty shy at first and he might not have contacted me if he had had to use the phone. He asked a friend for my number and a few days later he sent me a text: Gr8 2 meet U. I_/I_/? [drinks for two?]. I sent him a text message back and told him I'd love to see him again and that was how we arranged our first date.

"Text messaging is great for flirting and dating, it's less threatening for guys to get in touch to see if there is any interest. It's easier for them than calling to ask us out and that's got to be a good thing for everyone," enthused Amber. We agree with her—anything that lets people feel relaxed and good about flirting is great.

Flirting with text message can be both creative and witty, but not usually subtle, which is perhaps why it is popular. Although the text message sender might plead they were only joking or they didn't mean what you thought, text messages are easy to understand so long as you know the language. Here are some of our favorite flirty text messages:

{U}	hug U
('}{')	kissing
:) (: L8R?	meet later?
QTE	cutie
Cant W8 2 CU	Can't wait to see you

How to Flirt Using Text Messaging

Text message flirting can be fun and, as we've said, it is bold and direct. By remembering a few of the rules for general flirting, you can ensure your text message will be well received.

Don't try to be too smart. Unless you are already into more intimate sexual flirtations with someone, keep it light and playful rather than being overly suggestive.

Remember to flatter the person with something like URA* (you are a star). If they have done something for which you want to show appreciation, QTE (cutie) will let them know you find them attractive and can't be misinterpreted.

Like any other form of flirting, when you send a text message look for a response to your messages which indicates the receiver is enjoying the attention. With text messaging make sure they give you some encouragement with their responses.

If there is a risk with sending text messages, it's the risk of going overboard and sending a message that upsets or angers someone. We know of a potential romance that was cut short through a text message exchange.

Kate and Stuart met last December just before Kate flew off to spend Christmas with her family. While hundreds of miles apart they stayed in touch by exchanging text messages and continued what had started out as a fun flirtation. One night as Kate was about to go to bed another text message came from Stuart. Kate responded and they sent text messages back and forth for about an hour. Kate then got a message she did not expect. While she wouldn't tell us what Stuart had said in the text message she did say, "If he had ever said that to my face I would have slapped him." Instead she turned off her phone and went to bed and as far as we know, that was the end of their budding relationship.

So a word of caution: when sending a flirtatious text message remember to be playful, fun and light-hearted—and perhaps a little saucy if the situation calls for it.

Text Message Dictionary

The best Web site we found for text message text translations was http://lingo2word.com. It had the most comprehensive list of symbols, abbreviations and acronyms. Below are a few of our favorites.

Text Message	Meaning
2	To/too
4	For
8	Ate
+ly	Positively
2day	Today
2moro	Tomorrow
2nite	Tonight
3sum	Threesome
6Y	Sexy
AFAIK	As far as I know
AAMOF	As a matter of fact
B4	Before
BCNU	Be seeing you
BFN	Bye for now
BRT	Be right there
BTW	By the way
BYKT	But you knew that
C	See/sea
CIO	Check it out
CUL8R	See you later
CMIIW	Correct me if I'm wrong
D8	Date
EOL	End of lecture

EVRY1	Everyone
EZ	Easy
F8	Fate
FITB	Fill in the blank
FWIW	For what it's worth
FYI	For your information
GR8	Great
GTG	Got to go
H8	Hate
HTH	Hope this helps
IAC	In any case
IDK	I didn't know
IM @ WK	I'm at work
IMO	In my opinion
IMCO	In my considered opinion
IMHO	In my humble opinion
IOW	In other words
IUC	If you can
IYD	In your dreams
ILBL8	I'll be late
L8	Late
LOL	Laughing out loud
LMAO	Laughing my ass off
LMK	Let me know
MBRSD	Embarrassed
MSG	Message
NE	Any
NE1	Anyone
NO1	No one

NRN	No reply necessary
OIC	Oh I see
OTOH	On the other hand
OVR8D	Overrated
PC	Please Call
PLS	Please
?	Question
?ABLE	Questionable
R	Are
ROFL	Rolling on the floor laughing
RSN	Real soon now
RUOK	Are you OK?
SITD	Still in the dark
SPK	Speak
SUP	What's up?
THX	Thanks
TIA	Thanks in advance
TIC	Tongue in cheek
TTYL	Talk to you later
TUVM	Thank you very much
U	You
WB	Write back
WKND	Weekend
WOT	What?
XLNT	Excellent
Y	Why?
YNK	You never know
ZZZ	Sleeping
<G>	Grinning

<J>	Joking
<L>	Laughing
<S>	Smiling

Some Flirting Text Messages

HOT4U	Hot for you
I LYK U	I like you
U R 0–0	You are cool
U R 2 QT 2B 4GOTN	You are too cute to be forgotten
2 6Y	Too sexy
U R A QT	You are a cutie
U R A*	You are a star

Text message symbols have been taken from e-mail symbols and are usually used to express emotions after a comment or by way of responding to a message. Here are some symbols that you may find useful in flirting. Unless both people are aware of the meaning of the symbols, however, it can get mighty confusing.

SMS	Meaning
:-) or :)	Smile (joke)
(-:	Also smiling
(:-P	Oops
:-))	Very happy
:')	Happy and crying
:-D	Laughter
;-)	Wink
:-* or X	Kiss
{U}	Hug U
(')}{(')	Kissing

:)(: L8R?	Meet later?
I_/I_/	Drinks for two
;& or :-&	Tongue tied
@}—\-,—-	A rose
:-(	Sad
:'-(	Crying
:-c	Unhappy
:[	Very unhappy
:-||	Angry
:-(0)	Shouting
:-O	Uh oh or Wow
:I	Indifference
O :-)	An angel
:Q	Confused
:-9	Salivating
:-<>	Surprised
:-( )	Shocked
:@	Screaming
:-~)	Having a cold
:-o zz	Bored
:-\	Skeptical
:-o	Appalled
:-X	Not saying a word
|-I	Sleeping
%-}	Intoxicated
:-v	Talking

Text Message Strategy

The strategic use of text message technology can turn a simple meeting into a flirtation. For example, you meet someone innocently enough and by some pretense you get their card or their number. Later that day you send them a text message, which goes something like: "Gr8 to meet you & looking fwd to the nxt time," or "Thanx for the coffee & company," or "Mmm food 4 thought," or "Thinking of an xcuse to CU again."

Any message along these lines sends a clear message of appreciation and sets the mood for future flirting.

On-line and E-mail Flirting

In Victorian times a man and a women would have to be introduced. The woman, if she was interested, would agree to let the man formally call on her, which was considered to be courtship. The flirting continued with scented love letters passed back and forth.

Internet chatrooms and dating Web sites are now the hotbeds of flirting. You meet someone, something grabs your attention and you make an initial connection. Many people have said they prefer this way of flirting because they feel they can really get to know a person before actually meeting. By exchanging e-mails, they share their thoughts, feelings and passions without the pressure of physical contact.

There are many success stories of romances that started as e-mail flirtations and some of these romances have even led to marriage, but there are just as many disappointments when people realize they have fallen in love with a fantasy. *You've Got Mail* starred Tom Hanks and Meg Ryan as two people who "in real life" disliked each other but fell in love via e-mails. This movie showed us the potential for flirting via e-mail with someone you haven't met.

Strategies for Flirting Via E-mail

The seven flirting skills we spoke about early in the book can be applied equally on-line as they can in the flesh. You need to basically get in step with the other person to build rapport. Ask questions: what is the person interested in, what do they feel about . . . ? This is an excellent opportunity to really connect with their interests; a good question here might be, "I'm always curious about what people are interested in. What excites you?" Be creative. The Net is overflowing with jokes and funny pictures. Use something appropriate to liven up your e-mails.

In e-mail the verbal pause is impossible, but you can choose to only partially answer a question or leave a topic hanging so that they come back to you, thus indicating their interest and commitment to the flirting.

Paying compliments should not be forgotten, even electronically. If they send you a photo, compliment them on how they look. For example, Jay and Dana met on-line. Things were going pretty well and Jay convinced Dana to send him a photo. Dana eventually sent a photo of herself between her two uncles. Jay's response was, "Which one are you?" Dana's reply was silence.

On-line humor is tricky when you don't know the person well.

If you do choose to meet with your on-line buddy then the flirting is going to be pretty intense as you have probably already discussed your respective intentions: friendship, short-term, long-term relationships, etc. A word of advice: start from scratch and don't try to continue on from your last e-mail. There is whole new dynamic that arises when you meet in the flesh, so start slow and feel your way.

Telephone Flirting

While text messaging and e-mail can be fun and flirty, don't let them totally take the place of phone calls. If you find it works for you, text message until you feel the time is right to pick up the phone. Telephone flirting is powerful and can set you up for some great flirting experiences when you are face to face. It is one of the best and easiest ways we know to practice your flirting language and flirting listening skills.

Telephone flirting is multi-dimensional and differs from text message, chatrooms and e-mails because you are actually talking with someone. Talking involves more than just the words you use. It relies on your voice tone, inflections, the speed at which you speak, laughter and other emotional responses which deliver your messages to the other person. When you speak, you can make the listener feel and understand and respond to the conversation by more than the words you use.

Can you remember feeling encouraged or seduced by the sound of someone's voice? When any interaction is limited by the removal of one of the two channels (sight and sound), the other sense is heightened and your imagination fills in the gaps. How many times have you spoken to someone over the telephone and thought, "Wow, what a great voice." You paint a picture in your mind of how they look based on your reaction to what they say, how they say it and how the two of you are relating. Then you start flirting a little bit and if they respond to the flirting pretty soon you are in full flirt mode.

Telephone flirting is great for using the double entendre and painting some memorable pictures in your companion's mind. If you don't already use telephone flirting, start practising. Next time you get one of those telemarketing sales calls, don't hang up; use it as an opportunity to practise.

Telephone flirting can be great in business. You'll achieve a lot more just by using a little flirting in almost any circumstance. Getting someone's attention by schmoozing them and flirting will usually have a good outcome and makes both people feel good about the encounter. Dean adopted this attitude when he was chasing up a new credit card that had not arrived. Sure he was frustrated, but he chose to tackle the problem more creatively.

Dean had ordered the new card because the strip on his old one had worn out. The bank said they would post it to him. After ten days he had still not received the new card, so he called the bank. Instead of being angry with the person who took his call, Dean flirted. The result was that the girl he spoke to arranged to have the card sent to a branch close to where Dean worked.

Dean wasn't the only one who knew how to flirt because the next day the following telephone conversation took place:

"Hi, Dean, this is Lisa from [XYZ] bank . . ."

"You have my credit card," interrupted Dean excitedly.

"Yes," said Lisa flirtatiously. "I have it right here in my hot sticky hand."

"Well then, I will hotfoot it over," replied a breathless Dean.

They both laughed.

Dean's few moments on the phone with Lisa show how telephone flirting can be the source of great fun. Do you think Dean wanted to get to the bank to check out Lisa? She drew him a visual picture and he responded to it. It brightened both their days and the outcome made them both feel good. Like text message flirting, telephone flirting is often bolder than flirting face to face.

When you are flirting over the telephone there is a useful delay between "meeting" someone and meeting them face to face. There is also the chance of using an active imagination to fan the flames of telephone flirting to make it a little more thought provoking. As in Dean's case, many potential problems will have been sorted out through the use of a little telephone flattery and flirting. Friendships and relationships can develop by people getting to know each other through the telephone as well as text messaging, e-mail or in an Internet chatroom.

With your new flirting skills developed from our early chapters you can now practice flirting from afar. It's a great confidence booster and it is not a rehearsal—it is the real thing. Even with the differences we've discussed in flirting from afar and flirting face to face, the more chances you get to use your new flirting skills, the better you'll become at flirting with confidence.

Key Points

- Out of sight flirting can break the ice.
- Stay in touch by text message, e-mail or phone.
- Prepare to be a little bolder when you flirt out of sight.
- If you've never met your out-of-sight flirting buddy remember, there is a whole new dynamic created when meeting in the flesh, so start slow and feel your way.

ELEVEN

Make 'Em Feel Good

Too much of a good thing is wonderful.

Mae West

Richard held court at a bar with three pretty girls. He was relaxed and chatty, frequently telling jokes that made the girls laugh. If you watched closely you might just spot a pattern. While Richard was flirting with all three girls he was particularly interested in Christine, the girl to his left. Each time she laughed or smiled Richard would touch her right elbow and flash a smile at her. Richard was making Christine feel good with a touch and a smile.

It is natural for the human brain to create associations. You might associate a campfire with toasting marshmallows or telling stories. Knowing this we can create positive associations and avoid setting up negative ones. Later that evening Richard maneuvered himself to be between Christine and her friends. He gently touched her elbow on exactly the same spot and said, "I have enjoyed the evening, you make me *feel good*, can we do it *again*?" Richard emphasized his words and in Christine's mind and body she heard, "feel good, again." These thoughts were clearly linked to Richard's smile.

You can make yourself really memorable using carefully chosen phrases, voice tone, touch or gesture when you notice somebody is feeling good. Alternatively, you can use words to put someone in a good mood and then create an association between the good mood and yourself.

Creating positive associations—the "feel good factor"—is the final skill in flirting. You will need to be taking notice and be ready to go for it, but trust us, it is fun and rewarding.

In chapter two we introduced you to the concept of attitudes, moods or states and how they fluctuate. You learned how to choose a mood or get into the state. The make 'em feel good skill is about leading someone else into a good mood or intensifying an existing one. Once you notice the other person is having a good time you can create a strong association between yourself and this feeling and you can trigger this association any time.

The skill depends on you being able to take notice of other people's moods. What do you do or say to shift their attitude in a positive direction? When you talk to someone or ask them questions about what they like to do and what their interests are (see chapter five) they create pictures and sounds in their head. Their body responds as if they are actually experiencing the very thing you are talking about. When this happens, they start to get the feel good factor.

You will notice this by their breathing, their facial expression or the tone of their voice. A skilled flirt will then help them intensify the feeling by getting them to fill in more detail, to get in touch with the experience. As they start to move toward a peak experience, create a link or an association. Examples of links are:

- nodding your head
- touching them lightly
- saying yes
- repeating a phrase they have used to describe the experience
- copying a gesture they have used.

Does the name Pavlov ring a bell? Pavlov was the founder of modern behavioral psychology. Pavlov did experiments with dogs where he showed that by ringing a bell when he served the dogs their food they linked the sound of the bell to the food. In the next stage of the experiment he rang the bell without serving the food and the dogs still produced saliva in preparation for eating. He was able to prove that a stimulus (the bell) created a response (salivating). Now before you think we are about to liken flirting to training dogs, relax. People are much more interesting.

Do you know someone who makes you feel good when they are around? What is it—a smile, a look, a phrase, a tone of voice, a tilt of the head, a touch? Answering this question will give you an idea how you can use the brain's natural tendency to make associations to charge up your flirting.

Just making someone feel good will automatically link the feeling to you but if you reinforce this with a phrase, a smile, a look and/or a touch the result will amaze you. Go on, try it—you'll be blown away.

Your Mission

At work or in a social situation, try to bond with someone. Notice their mood by watching their facial expression, breathing and posture changes. When they move into a positive mood, smile, nod and say, "Yes."

Keep doing this for at least ten minutes. Then when they are in a neutral mood, nod and say, "Yes." Stand back and watch the result.

As we have mentioned before, words have to be de-coded and processed to be understood. The very process of de-coding will lead the listener through the process of accessing the feelings. You can use language to invite people to experience various feelings. For example:

"Are you having fun?"
"Are you enjoying yourself?"
"It's okay to have fun."
"And enjoying yourself is good too."
"You are having fun, aren't you?"

The brain naturally makes links. Your unconscious mind is constantly asking, "What is this like?" and, "Where have I experienced this before?"

As each new thing happens to us we create links to previous thoughts and feelings. We are constantly trying to find the meaning in life and we do that by labeling, evaluating and associating events. Examples of verbal links might be:

"You smiling at me *means* you like me."
"Feeling a warm tingle around you *means* I like you."

Sometimes we create unhealthy links or phobias such as:

"All spiders are dangerous and are about to attack me."
"Entering a new social situation will *mean* embarrassment for me."

Understanding how to link someone feeling good to you is a great skill to have. If you want to use language to create good feelings then here are some magic words to help you do it.

- aware
- realize
- experience
- notice
- consider
- imagine.

They are all awareness verbs that cause the listener's brain to process whatever you say afterward. For example:

"I'm sure you are *aware* that you look sensational in that dress."
"Do you *realize* how lucky we are to be enjoying this sunset together?"

"Would you like to *experience* the passion of Latin dancing?"

"*Notice* how the wind in you hair makes you feel so free."

"*Consider* how special it is be able to chat so easily to someone you have just met."

"Can you *imagine* how much more fun we can have?"

You can use these words equally powerfully in questions or statements.

The language can either relate to what is actually going on (utilization) or create an expectation of what might be.

Using Awareness Verbs

Now it's your turn. Write out a couple of sentences for each awareness verb. You'll be surprised when you realize how much fun you can have making other people feel good. Imagine how your flirting will reach new levels and you'll have some experiences that will surprise and amaze you as a result.

More Ways to Link with Words

As we have mentioned, the brain is looking for links and associations. A good flirt won't leave these links to chance. Using the following words you can link a cause to an effect or imply that something leads to something else.

- and
- means
- as

- causes
- because.

Examples of this are:

- Drinking that brand of beer *means* you are a man of taste *and* would recognize quality when you see it [insert non-verbal here].
- *As* we talk I feel that we're really getting to know each other.
- Seeing you again *causes* me to think back to that wonderful little pub where we first met.
- Are you enjoying the coffee, *because* I wanted to make it special for you.

Using Cause/Effect Words

Write out a couple of sentences for each cause/effect word. As you write each sentence you'll feel increasingly flirtatious because practice means you are getting closer to your goal and causes growing excitement.

Au Revoir

It's not goodbye, it's *au revoir*. There is a pleasant side effect from being a great flirt—people want to be around you and may want more of you than you want to give. Learning to leave people feeling good about their time with you is an essential skill. The alternative is a burn-and-churn approach, which will earn you bad karma or an unsavory reputation.

One of the things we noticed when coaching people to flirt is that they could use their flirting skills to make contact easier than they expected.

A Night Out with *Flirting 101*

The media often contact us looking to do stories based on case studies of our work. A popular women's magazine asked if they could observe, interview and photograph a group of girls we had coached in flirting. The plan was to take four volunteers, who had previously had difficulty flirting, coach them on the basics and then set them loose in a busy city bar on a Friday night.

Participant number one, Louise, the magazine journalist, was out to get as much material for her article as possible, and was keen to test our flirting strategies rigorously.

Lisa was constantly being told she was beautiful but didn't believe it. This affected her self-esteem and the person she showed to the world.

Anna was shy and spent her time looking for a life partner. Her focus on this prevented her from meeting new guys because she was always judging them.

Karen had a boyfriend but wanted to learn how to flirt.

We met at a popular after-work drinking hole and were joined by Steve, the magazine's photographer.

After about 30 minutes of explaining flirting attitudes and practicing some basic skills we agreed they would not leave the bar with someone they met during the flirting game. No contact would last more than fifteen minutes and, most important, they would always disengage leaving the guys feeling good.

After the first fifteen-minute session we met up again and the girls were excited about their successes. Everyone had made eye contact with lots of people and exchanged smiles—all of them had managed to get hellos and conversations, and half the group had scored a phone number. Louise had told her new friend that she was doing a story and asked him to pose with her for a photo. He was a bit disappointed but was a good sport.

For round two we moved to the cocktail lounge. Here was a more challenging venue as most people were sitting down or milling around in small groups. With success under their belts our flirt students were ready to try some more overt signals such as walking past someone to get their attention or inclining their head to indicate an invitation to join them at a table. In no time all of them were in conversation with someone new.

All of the girls found the fifteen-minute time limit made them give lots of green lights to get results. What they hadn't anticipated was the strength of the positive response. Consequently, they often forgot how to pace their flirting and disengage gracefully.

The lesson to learn from this experience is that a good flirt always notices how the other person is feeling. Because the girls were so intent on practicing their verbal and non-verbal skills they forgot one of the core attitudes—taking notice—and the skill of making the other person feel good.

The misconception is that it's hard to meet people whereas the real challenge is not making the contact but flirting without the promise of more. This ensures both parties enjoy the flirting but don't expect something that's not being offered. Disengaging when you have made it clear that you are only flirting is as easy as saying, "Thank you, I have enjoyed talking with you."

At the end of the night, Anna, who had started out being very shy, came to life and, despite getting a couple of numbers, decided that Steve the photographer was more her type. She asked him for his number. Lisa, with her low self-esteem, had collected the most phone numbers and went home feeling good about herself. Karen spent time chatting to a pilot who was disappointed that the flirting had to stop there, but after Karen explained her objective they parted as friends. Louise was pleased with the material she got for the article but had not learned, or wanted, to disengage. She was last seen leaving the bar with two good-looking twenty-year-olds.

Connecting and disengaging when flirting was covered by the rules of etiquette in Victorian times, as we mentioned in chapter one. Robert Greene, in his book *The Art of Seduction*, recounts the story of Benjamin Disraeli, a prominent figure of these times. He dressed in colorful, flamboyant clothes, following all of the bizarre dandy fashions. He also wrote novels, flowery pieces of fiction that were the equivalent of his everyday dandy style. His stories were quite brilliant. And, on top of it all, Disraeli was not a very handsome man. In Victorian England it would be hard to imagine a more unlikely flirt. And yet Benjamin Disraeli had an irresistible effect on both men and women. There was his infamous wit, his indulgent, tolerant character, his unflappable calmness. Then there was his power of conversation. He would seem to listen to you with his whole body, understand your moods, reflect on your ideas.

One princess who fell under his spell wrote about

Disraeli and his great political opponent, William Glad-stone: "When I left the dining room after sitting next to Mr. Gladstone, I thought he was the cleverest man in England. But after sitting next to Mr. Disraeli, I thought I was the cleverest woman in England." He was a flirt and a charmer, and if you read his diaries you know that this was all a conscious and strategic plan.

Disraeli was elected to parliament, where he proceeded to charm his colleagues, becoming one of the most popu-lar members and eventually being elected head of the Tory (conservative) Party. And then, in 1871, this man, who was to all appearances an outsider, was elected Prime Minister of England—one of the most remarkable political feats of all time. As Prime Minister, Disraeli had to have constant, if not daily, contact with Queen Victoria. Two more dissimilar people could not be imagined. The Queen was stubborn, dour, insecure, prudish—the polar opposite of Disraeli. Now, a normal man in such a situation would struggle to tone down his flamboyant qualities, which would certainly rub Queen Victoria the wrong way. But Disraeli did the opposite—he raised his charm levels. He brazenly flirted with the Queen, sent her parliamen-tary notes that were more like love letters, called her pet names, sent her flowers, thoughtful gifts, adoring letters. In other words, he treated her like a woman he was courting.

Was the Queen repulsed, terrified, embarrassed? No, like everyone else she fell under his spell, only deeper than anyone else. The Queen quite simply fell in love. He not only made her feel like a desirable woman, but also a great and confident leader. She became his most ardent supporter, the bulwark of his power, eventually making him the Earl of Beaconsfield, a member of the peerage, the culmination of all his dreams.

The story of Disraeli illustrates the rewards of having the right attitude, being in the best mood, flirting fluently and making 'em feel good. Disraeli was also strategic in his approach and that is the topic of the next chapter.

Key Points

- Create a positive association between feeling good and yourself.
- Make the other person feel good about themselves.
- Pace your flirting.
- Disengage with style.

TWELVE

Strategic Flirting

Life consists not in holding good cards but in playing those you hold well.

Josh Billings

Do you need to have a strategy to flirt or is it just better to let it happen naturally? This is a question we have been asked countless times and the answer is that both work. Flirting is often spontaneous; you don't need to have a strategy to flirt successfully. Flirting is fun when it just happens because there are no expectations and no definitive outcomes in mind—except to have fun.

On the other hand, if you have a clear intention then flirting will help you reach your goal—it pays to have a strategy. The most common intention with flirting is to be noticed and that works equally well in business or in love. Take Jenny's story. She knew she wanted to meet Shawn, she just had to figure out how and when she could make it happen.

When we first met Jenny she was out at one of the city's popular bars chatting to a group of guys and looking like she was simply having fun. When we got to talk to her later, we found that this night had been planned with precision to make sure she got to meet Shawn. Jenny had seen Shawn at a party some weeks before and wanted to meet him, but he had taken a date to the party. Jenny decided to back off and do some detective work.

She knew people who knew Shawn so she started making some discreet enquiries. Through her research she found out that Shawn was single. She also discovered that she knew some of the group who hung out with him. She figured that if she tagged along with people who knew Shawn well, they'd all end up at the same place and, eventually, get around to introducing her to him. This is exactly what had happened.

Jenny started socializing more with people she knew were his friends. She was a bright, bubbly and fun addition to the group, so they were happy to keep inviting her to meet up with them. By doing this she started to cultivate new friendships but didn't get close to any one person. It took about three weeks before she finally got to meet Shawn. She had been introduced the night we saw her in the bar and was now chatting to him in an effort to get to know him better.

Over the previous few weeks, Jenny had been chatty and friendly to the other guys but didn't give out any flirting signals until she was introduced to Shawn. When she met him she started sending some clear signals of interest in his direction. When he responded by flirting back, Jenny's flirting went up a gear. She found Shawn's flirting became more direct and their body language was unmistakable. Leaning toward each other, giggling, whispering, casually touching to make a point, they were soon doing the flirting dance.

Jenny's goal to meet Shawn had been orchestrated with the precision of a military operation but seemed to be quite natural as she became part of the group that hung out together. Because Jenny had not flirted with other guys in the group, she made a distinction that was obvious to both Shawn and the other guys. Her strategy worked—it was clear to Shawn that Jenny's flirtatious comments were meant for him alone. Her well-thought-out strategies and careful planning had worked. When we last saw her, Jenny and Shawn had been together almost a year and were about to move in together.

Now don't get us wrong—we do not recommend stalking! There is a line that should never be crossed. We've heard of a company that will find out everything about your romantic target for you, arrange for "accidental" meetings so that you'll be at the same party or seated next to the unsuspecting bunny on a plane. A master flirt would *not do this*. This is not about making somebody feel special, it's about satisfying a personal fantasy and it could get you arrested!

There is a big difference between stalking and taking opportunities to "run into" someone you're interested in.

For instance, you might take notice when and where that someone has coffee and just happen to be there—that is strategic. Hanging outside their place with binoculars is sick.

While you can flirt with just about anyone, you will choose to flirt with some people and not with others. While it is also possible to flirt with more than one person at a time, group flirting is a bit like doing (almost) anything in a group—not quite as much fun and nowhere near as subtle as one on one. Choosing who to flirt with is a bit like selecting which chocolate you are going to have from an assorted box. Everyone has their favorite. You might prefer the coffee cream or the almond praline so you choose this one, pop it into your mouth and enjoy the taste sensation as it coats the inside of your mouth. Sure, you might go on and have another one, but you have taken the time to savor the first. Think of how the experience would change if you grabbed a handful of mixed chocolates and shoveled them into your mouth at the same time. All the flavors would get mixed together and their subtleties would be lost in a mass of chocolate and cream and nuts and cherry liqueur and toffee.

How do you select who to flirt with? It depends on a mix of how someone looks, their energy level and an almost unconscious synergy. Previous experiences will have given you feedback on how your flirting is likely to be received by certain types of people. As you now have a greater sense of self, you might discover the focus of your selection will have shifted. Now that you've decided to become a master flirt, you'll start paying more attention to who you flirt with and the results you get. In time both your skills and your intuition will reach new levels.

Jane never thought of herself as a flirt and yet everyone

who heard her spend time on the phone talking to clients knew she was in fact great at it. "Ooh," she said when she heard about our work. "Please can I have some tips?"

"We're not sure you need any," we said flirtatiously.

"Well, I guess I have been working on it."

"How do you know who to flirt with?" we asked.

"It's how they sound. There's a certain something in the voice that lets me know it's okay to flirt, so I say something cheekily and see how they respond."

What is it that lets you flirt with someone? Is it their facial expressions? Is it the way they seem to be relating to those around them? Is it an energy thing? What is it for you?

Take some time to think about the people you have flirted with recently. When flirting strategically you need to have a clear idea of who you want to flirt with and the result you want. To do this you need to get yourself into the right attitude, into the right place at the right time, and be prepared to send the right signals. The strategic flirter is aware they need to pace the action by using the right non-verbal signals and the right flirtatious language.

Strategic Intentions

It is important to know your intention when flirting strategically, as your intentions will drive your results. If you have an intention but don't have a plan, you may be misunderstood and the results could range from humorous to disastrous. So what is your intention when you flirt? Here is a checklist before you let the magic loose, but bear in mind that these are only some of the reasons why you may flirt.

- Is it an extension of my personality?
- Is it to make other people feel special, to brighten up their day?
- Is it to check out an available partner for a relationship?
- Is it to get laid?
- Is it to lighten a difficult situation?
- Is it to create a good impression?
- Is it to do business?

When your flirting has an intended outcome you'll want to be very clear on the what, the why, the when and the how. The "what" is your goal or intended outcome. This could be getting noticed, a date or a coveted business contract. The "why" is what motivates you to go for your goal. How motivated you are will determine how patient and persistent you'll be. The "when" is about timing. It's picking the right time, the right situation and knowing how to pace the flirting. It's the "how" that is your strategy, your plan of action and the steps you'll take.

Your "how to" strategy will include the methods of flirting you think best suit the situation. Are you going to be more effective face to face or text messaging, using the telephone, e-mail or a combination of all four? The how is also about putting some foundations in place, as Jenny did by becoming part of the group that would get her an introduction to Shawn.

Hunting in Packs

Many people we have spoken to and observed prefer to
do their flirting in packs. A group of single girlfriends or
a group of guys will head off to the pub, the beach or some
other popular meeting place. The advantage of this
strategy is twofold: first, you have the support of your
friends to help judge your target's suitability and to egg
you on to make contact; second, strategic flirting alone
can be risky and can make you look desperate, and that
is just not attractive.

People are drawn to groups that are having a lot of
fun. They want to be a part of the fun. So how does it
work? Here is a common scenario: A group of girlfriends
goes for after-work drinks. They have fun chatting and
catching up. One of the girls spies a guy in a group of
men who she thinks is "cute." She alerts her friends who
"check him out" and his "cuteness" goes to a group vote.
If the group agree they ramp up their interest to "you
go, girl." Eye contact is initiated and then the next bit
comes down to timing. Eventually the "cute guy" is going
to buy another drink, so the "interested girl" is just going
to be at the bar at the same time. More eye contact and
an "accidental" brush against his arm means the "cute
guy" is getting the green light. Before long the two groups
of friends are starting to mingle and the flirting continues.

Boys in packs will often use the same strategy but have
to be careful not to be overpowering or seem macho. There
is a great scene in *A Beautiful Mind* where a stunning
blonde and her friends arrive in the bar. All the boys except
the John Nash character salivate over her and become
competitive, trying to figure out how they can get the

advantage and score the blonde. This situation is the catalyst for John Nash's theory of governing dynamics. He explains to them that if they all go for the blonde, they'll block each other and none of them will score her. If, after failing, they then go for her friends, the friends will give them the cold shoulder as nobody likes to be second best. He further explains that if nobody goes for the blonde but go for her friends instead, they will all get laid. Remarkably, considering his lack of social skill, John Nash recognized that to be successful sometimes flirting requires a strategy.

Everyone will have their own flirting strategy but they are often unaware of what it is. When we did our initial research Jill told us about her friend Rachel who in her opinion had a great flirting strategy. When we spoke to Rachel she had no idea what her strategy was. However, when we interviewed Renee and Trent, both self-confessed master flirts, they willingly revealed strategies, beliefs and attitudes about their flirting approach.

First we asked them about strategic intentions—the "what" and the "why" of flirting. Then we were curious about the "when" and "how."

What is your intention when you flirt?

Renee: With me it's an energy thing. When I meet someone with the right kind of energy I like to play. It's not always sexual as I flirt with both women and men. What I always do is focus on their number one interest: themselves. When there is a mutual attraction with a man I will make it very clear to him that I want to get to know him better. I will try different flirting techniques and I'm a little suggestive, so the message and intention are clear. My intent when I flirt is to awaken feelings in another person, to be playful. I like to take them to the edge of their comfort zone in a light and fun way, to make their day better by introducing a bit of play time and lightness.

Trent: Flirting for me is about the male–female interplay. It does have sexual overtones so I don't flirt with other men. I use being cheeky and flirtatious to get somewhere or get something done—so if I want to get upgraded on a flight or need help at the bank, I'll always pick a female attendant. Take the airport for example—I play dumb, in need of help, so I appeal to their sense of importance—I make them feel good about themselves.

When do you flirt?
Renee: Whenever and wherever I can. Flirting belongs almost anywhere if it is in a fun, light-hearted manner because it makes everyone feel good. I also use flirting to enhance communication with someone. Flirting opens up the conversation and lightens the mood. I don't use flirting consciously to get something from others, although I find that the more attention I pay to someone the more attention I get. I get better service, the best table in a restaurant, an upgrade. People are more willing to help me in every area.

Trent: When I'm trying to bend or break a rule, I need to get the person making the decision to work *with* me. On the phone is great because I can work with their imagination. There are two situations where I flirt: flirting for outcome—a relationship or sex—or flirting for sport— just for fun. We both enjoy it but there's no intent.

How do you flirt? What strategies do you use?
Renee: Strategies depend on the situation, the person and desired outcome. They could be as subtle as sustained eye contact to grabbing onto a man's arm, looking into his eyes and telling him how strong he feels. I know that's obvious, but guys love it. Overall, it is about taking interest in the other person and listening so intently that you block out all other distractions. It's about asking questions, asking why and getting into the heart and soul of the other person. If chemistry is involved, it's about catching my breath, smiling a subtle, maybe slightly suggestive smile, being acutely conscious of body language, of standing closer than normal, almost touching but not quite, then emphasizing a point with a brief touch on their arm, hand or, if I'm feeling really adventurous, their leg! The most powerful flirting I have experienced is via e-mail. Incredible intimacy can be created and honest communication opened up because of the seeming anonymity of the medium and ease of dialogue. Innuendo, double meanings, it is such fun!

Trent: I smile. I'm subtle and use eye contact and lots of humor. It's very important to get them to like you and I use humor because it disarms people and allows them to feel safe and confident. I use wit for genuine engagement and I'm not the type to send messages across the room. I'm up close and personal, I move in first, read the vibes, then flirt if it's appropriate. My strength is in the interaction so I can't do that at a distance.

What flirting strategies do you use?
Trent: I'm an opportunist in life so my strategy is always built around the opportunity someone has presented to

me—a look, something they say. I use humor as a hook and look at body language. Flirting requires an awareness of others. I also engage at the level of what the woman is doing. I don't begin with a verbal compliment—what lovely eyes you have, etc. I affirm them as a person so they drop their guard. If I chat first, then compliment her eyes later, it works far better because I've already engaged her and don't sound so superficial. But I have to pick that moment carefully because timing is everything.

With any strategy it is as important to know when not to use it, so we asked.

Is there any situation where you won't flirt?
Renee: Every situation and individual is unique. I hold back from flirting when I am pitching for business, although I suspect it is so ingrained in me that I unconsciously flirt in some subtle way all the time.

Trent: Absolutely. I don't flirt where there is accountability. I'll only flirt with friends if they know it's safe and fun. I'd never flirt in a group of friends for sport when something could go wrong and I'd wreck the friendships. For me, flirting needs to be without consequence so I can just walk away if it is not going well. It has a lot to do with awareness. If you don't pick up on the vibes, you'll be a hopeless flirt.

You can see that Renee and Trent are confident about themselves as flirts, and are aware of the strategies they use. They both have a strategy for flirting and they agree that it makes their lives fun, playful and they score a few fringe benefits.

Since you may not know what your flirting moves are, get a friend to answer the following questions for you, but first pour both of you a nice big drink as this is going to be lots of fun. Check off any answers that apply.

How would your friend describe you as a flirt:
❑ master flirt
❑ great flirt
❑ flirts all the time
❑ doesn't flirt often
❑ is too shy to flirt
❑ flirts with everyone
❑ only flirts if someone starts flirting with you
❑ only flirts with someone you really dig

When you flirt are the situations:
❑ business
❑ social
❑ pub or club
❑ public place
❑ beach
❑ anywhere
❑ other

How were you dressed:
❑ casual
❑ grunge
❑ smart
❑ sexy
❑ formal

❑ swimwear
❑ other

How did you make your selection:
❑ looks
❑ voice
❑ they showed interest in you
❑ someone introduced you
❑ other

What non-verbal signals did you use:
❑ the scan (the room-encompassing glance)
❑ hello, hello (the short darting glance)
❑ lock and load (the fixed gaze)
❑ smiling
❑ eyebrow flash
❑ hey, look at me
❑ approach
❑ come on over
❑ solitary dance
❑ toss, tilt and laugh
❑ hair flip
❑ look, I'm vulnerable
❑ the whisper
❑ fondling things (caressing objects)
❑ the brush
❑ the lean
❑ the touch
❑ the foot to foot, knee to knee or thigh to thigh

❑ play
❑ hugs
❑ kissing
❑ other

How did you get in step with the person:
❑ use of language
❑ mirroring and matching
❑ asking questions
❑ humor
❑ other

Did you give all green lights or do you use stop/go?
Do you close the gap?
Do you withdraw and watch what happens?
Is there somewhere you would never flirt?

What's Your Strategy?

What is your intention when you flirt?
When do you flirt?
What types of flirting do you use?
Do you know when not to?

Flirting in a Relationship

What happens when flirting does lead to a relationship?
Do you stop flirting with your partner? Do you stop
flirting with other people?

A great flirt never stops flirting with their partner. If flirting is about playful energy and making the other person feel acknowledged, complimented and appreciated, why would you ever stop?

Flirting with your partner follows the same steps we have been talking about throughout this book. In a relationship you can take flirting a lot deeper and obviously further because there is the added dimension of a sexual intimacy.

Rob and his wife Isabelle still flirt with each other as much as they ever did. They were going out for drinks with friends one Friday night and as he left for work in the morning he said, "Are you thinking of wearing that short black skirt tonight, Bella?" When she asked, "Why are you interested in what I might or might not have on tonight?" he laughed at her question and told her, "Because if you *are* thinking of wearing that skirt, I'll spend my day thinking about your sensational legs." They both spent their day in pleasurable anticipation of the night ahead.

They whetted each other's appetite by being flirtatiously playful—their flirting enhanced their mood and got them both feeling appreciated, sensual and sexy. For Rob and Isabelle, the flirting keeps their relationship fun and alive and they never forget how to be playful with each other.

Putting It All Together

Imagine how your life will be different now as you sprinkle a little flirting magic into your day-to-day interactions. Think about how you will get better service in stores and restaurants because you flirt with the staff, more cheerful help because you ask with a smile and a little flirting, a better response to the requests you make because you are able to step into the other person's shoes. As a great flirt you are fearless when talking to people, whether for the first or umpteenth time. When you meet someone you want to flirt with you know how to get in step, to ask an engaging question. Now it's time to put it all together, the flirting attitude, the flirting skills and your own touch of uniqueness to be a playful, light-hearted flirt—anywhere and everywhere you can.

Key Points

- Great flirts strategize when there is something or someone they want.
- Great flirts know why, what, when and how.
- Great flirts know what techniques to use when and where.
- Great flirts put it together with style.

About the Authors

Andrew Bryant is a speaker, trainer and coach, and founder of communication consultancy Self Leadership International. Initially trained as a physiotherapist, Andrew has a strong background in the fields of health and communication, including acupuncture, hypnosis, neuro-linguistics and neuro-semantics.

Originally from England, Andrew arrived in Australia in 1985 on a working visa and decided to stay. Andrew is passionate about teaching and coaching people to "manage their minds" in order to obtain maximum enjoyment out of life.

The idea for this book grew from one of Andrew's seminars in 2002, Flirting for Business and Pleasure. In fact, it was Andrew's events manager at that time who first suggested the topic, as she had found, through her own experiences, that there were a lot of people who could do with some communication training to improve their flirting techniques.

Andrew's research led him to believe that there was a simple and practical way of teaching people how to flirt.

The two-hour seminar was a moderate success but the bonus for Andrew was learning a lot about what people needed to know to make them comfortable with the idea and practice of flirting.

The fun for Andrew was in field-testing the techniques. The first time he took a group he had coached to a trendy city bar on a Friday night he was slightly nervous, not knowing if he had taught them enough or how well they would do. The results were amazing. Men and women who were previously shy of the opposite sex were walking up to strangers and making meaningful contact. It was then he realized—this stuff works!

Michelle Lia Lewis spent eight years as a matchmaker with Australia's leading introduction agency, counseling clients on dating and relationships, and has listened to the best and worst flirts talk about their experiences.

When Michelle arranged a date for a client she always looked forward to the feedback. Sure, it was part of her job, but there was more to it than that—she had, and still has, a passion for charting patterns of behavior that worked, and those that flopped. Although she didn't know it at the time, those clients were preparing her for the writing of this book. She discovered early in her match-making career that success most often came to those who took a positive attitude into each meeting and didn't put too much emphasis on the other person being "the one" for them—they went into each date prepared to enjoy meeting someone new. Michelle also learned how much it helped when a client got out of their own shoes, meta-phorically speaking, and into those of the other person, and really tried to understand them.

Flirting follows the same rule, so when Andrew was looking for a coauthor, Michelle was a natural choice.

Michelle has appeared as a matchmaker, relationship adviser and commentator in the Channel 9 series *Single Girls* in 2000. She has been quoted on relationships in numerous publications, including *WHO Weekly, B Magazine, New Woman, Body+Soul* in *The Sunday Telegraph* and *Sunday Life* and *S* in *The Sun-Herald*. Michelle is the founder of datedoctors.com, a relationship counseling service. She divides her time among freelance writing, consulting and working on a concept for a new television dating program. She was an advice columnist for *B Magazine* and is now the relationship adviser and expert for shesaid.com.au, answering reader's questions and writing articles.

We'd love to hear your flirting stories and would be happy to answer your flirting questions. Visit Andrew at www.flirting.net.au and Michelle at www.datedoctors.com or email us at michelle@datedoctors.com or andrew@ flirting.net.au.